D0519246

MEL&SUE

Tina Campanella is an award-winning former tabloid and magazine journalist, as well as the author of books about British Comedy Award-winning Sarah Millican, tennis star Laura Robson, and the boyband Union J. She lives in North London with her partner, artist Russell Marshall, and their dog Alfie. You can tweet her at @littlebell1982.

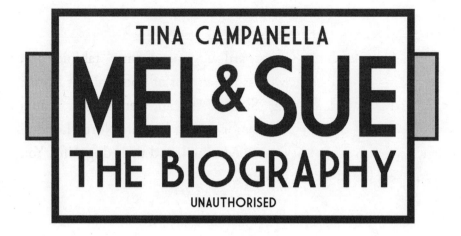

TINA CAMPANELLA

MEL&SUE
THE BIOGRAPHY
UNAUTHORISED

JOHN BLAKE

Published by John Blake Publishing Ltd,
3 Bramber Court, 2 Bramber Road,
London W14 9PB, England

www.johnblakepublishing.co.uk

www.facebook.com/johnblakebooks ◼
twitter.com/jblakebooks ◼

First published in hardback in 2014

ISBN: 978-1-78418-012-6

All rights reserved. No part of this publication may be reproduced, stored in a
retrieval system, or transmitted in any form or by any means, without the prior
permission in writing of the publisher, nor be otherwise circulated in any form
of binding or cover other than that in which it is published and without a similar
condition including this condition being imposed on the subsequent purchaser.

British Library Cataloguing-in-Publication Data:

A catalogue record for this book is available from the British Library.

Design by www.envydesign.co.uk

Printed in Great Britain by CPI Group (UK) Ltd

3 5 7 9 10 8 6 4 2

© Text copyright Tina Campanella 2014

The right of Tina Campanella to be identified as the author of this work has been
asserted by her in accordance with the Copyright, Designs and Patents Act 1988.

Papers used by John Blake Publishing are natural, recyclable products made from
wood grown in sustainable forests. The manufacturing processes conform to the
environmental regulations of the country of origin.

Every attempt has been made to contact the relevant copyright-holders,
but some were unobtainable. We would be grateful if the appropriate people
could contact us.

CONTENTS

PROLOGUE

If you were a student during the 1990s there's one daytime programme you'll not have missed: Channel 4's *Light Lunch*.

Coming from seemingly out of nowhere, its two refreshingly different presenters reduced the country to fits of laughter. With their extra servings of boundless energy and awful puns, Mel Giedroyc and Sue Perkins soon turned the light-hearted cookery chat show into a staple part of the British TV diet.

But as quickly as their fame had risen, it soon began to sink: quitting the show that had made them household names they decided to take their double act down a number of different celebrity paths, but none of them replicated the success they'd first achieved with *Light Lunch*.

Finally they split, going their separate ways to seek their own recognition. It would be nearly a decade before the country tucked into a Mel and Sue comedy feast once again: in the form of the instant BBC hit show, *The Great British Bake Off*.

Hotting up and cooling down, and with a few buns in the oven in between, this is the story of Britain's new favourite female comedy duo and the complicated road they walked to becoming the nation's sweethearts they are today.

CHAPTER 1

MEET MEL...

*'The only way to get attention was to throw yourself off the top of a
ladder – as one of my cousins used to do – or make people laugh...'*
Mel Giedroyc, quoted in *The Guardian*, 2012

Melanie Clare Sophie Giedroyc was born on 5 June 1968
in the market town of Epsom, Surrey. Growing up the
youngest of four in a lively, bustling household, from the moment
Mel could talk it was clear that she would have to work hard just
to get a word in edgeways: but in hindsight, with such a confident
and talented set of older siblings to inspire her, Mel was always
going to be a success.

Her elder sister by six years, Mary-Rose Helen (known as
Coky) Giedroyc is now an acclaimed and award-winning film
and TV director. She is best known for her work directing
British television dramas such as *Wuthering Heights*, *Carrie's
War* and *Oliver Twist* and was nominated for a BAFTA for *The
Virgin Queen*. She is married to baronet Sir Thomas Weyland
Bowyer-Smyth, making her official title the rather grand Lady
Bowyer-Smyth.

Mel's other sister, Kasia, is the wife of British diplomat Philip John Parham and is a teacher, author and champion of children's rights. She is the author/editor of the *Teach Africa* book series, which aims to educate British children about the developing world.

Elder brother Miko is a respected musician and composer who has written for *The Spectator*. And mother, Rosy, is an artist, but amidst all the family-life creative din, Mel steadfastly forged her pathway to individuality by making everyone laugh.

'When you're the youngest of a large, exhibitionist family, you have to do something to get your parents' attention,' she has explained to *The Daily Mail*. 'I was pretty goofy and got all the hand-me-down clothes. I looked like a boy – short hair, very small, big teeth – you've got to go for the gags.'

It's not surprising then, that although she had a happy childhood, she admits she was an extremely competitive child, with a prodigious work ethic that would continue to serve her well throughout her life.

But while Mel's early life sounds about as middle class and English as you can get, you'd be deceived if you were to think that her family was that comfortingly normal: in fact, their story is much more interesting than that.

The Giedroyc family's strong work ethic comes from their father, and originally stems from a part of Mel's history that wasn't openly or explicitly discussed until relatively recently: her father Michal's astounding early life.

There is a clue in her name, which looks beautifully complicated to pronounce (it's *Ged-roych*) and is certainly unusual in the showbiz world. Most people with an even vaguely exotic real moniker give themselves a simpler, more catchy stage name early on in their careers: Demetria Guynes became Demi Moore,

Krishna Pandit Bhanji changed his name to Ben Kingsley, and Georgios Panayiotou transformed into George Michael.

But Mel is proud of her family name, and rightly so – there was no way she was going to change it, especially once she learnt about its proud heritage: the Giedroyc family is descended from a very distinguished line of medieval Lithuanian noblemen. Mel herself is the seventeenth-generation grandchild of Prince Bartlomiej of Lithuania, prominent member of the country's sixteenth-century Grand Duchy.

As a child, Mel's father Michal lived on a grand manor house estate in Poland, the treasured son of Polish war hero Tadeusz Giedroyc, who, after winning numerous medals for valour, had been made a Senator of the Second Polish Republic.

But the now critically-acclaimed historian has just a few scant physical reminders of this prestigious heritage, among which are some of the family silver (two forks and two spoons), which his mother managed to save, and a prayer book given to him on his first communion.

Michal had lived a peaceful early life riding horses and playing with his pet dogs until the onset of the Second World War turned the family's charmed life upside down. Aged just 10 when the war broke out in 1939 he could only watch in horror as his brave father was taken away to be tortured and imprisoned in Minsk. He would never see him again.

Michal, along with his mother and two sisters, was also dragged from the affluent family seat in Lobzow, East Poland, by the invading Soviet Army. Their beloved home was subsequently razed to the ground. Banned from taking any personal belongings, and newly designated as 'enemies of the people', they were dispatched by train in a sealed cattle-truck to Siberia.

The subsequent two-week journey was almost indescribably hellish. There were no toilet facilities, just a hole in the floor, which they shared with more than 40 other people. Once a day they were given water; once a week food. They were treated as less than human.

Michal and his family sat by a window for fresh air, and it was from there that he saw the prison where his father was being held, as the train passed slowly through Minsk. In Siberia they were locked up in horrific work camps – a far cry from the life they had known and treasured in Poland.

It was just the start of an odyssey that Mel had always heard stories about – 'I only gave you anecdotes,' her father told her many years later – but didn't know the full horrific detail of for decades. And it was a journey that would both define Michal's life and instil in all of his children a powerful world view.

'There is definitely a strength in all of us as a family,' Mel said to the *Daily Express* in 2010. 'I have a strong need to achieve things for myself and I think that comes from him.'

For just over two years, the pre-teen Michal and his family were forced to perform backbreaking manual labour, which swiftly overcame most of their fellow captives, who perished around them from hunger and neglect.

Miraculously, Michal and the Giedroyc women survived the ordeal and were eventually released and deported, as war continued to tear Europe apart. Destitute and half-starved, the family could only attempt to walk their way through uncertain territory to find some kind of safety. But as terrifying and difficult as this must have been, Michal's father had not been so lucky.

Unbeknownst to his anxious family, after two years of unimaginable torture, Tadeusz was shot at the side of a road by retreating Russian soldiers in 1941 – a heartbreaking end that went undiscovered by the Giedroycs for seven years.

'It must be very hard for a fatherless boy to make his way in the shadow of such horrific events,' Mel said in the same interview with the *Daily Express*, whilst explaining that she only fully began comprehending the immensity of her father's ordeal once she became an adult.

In temperatures of minus 20, wearing ragged clothes and with no food, Michal and his remaining family began a long, dangerous and unpredictable journey. Passing through Persia and Iraq, traversing most of Soviet Central Asia, they eventually arrived in Iran, when Michal was 15. There he joined the Free Polish Army and became a soldier just like his father – desperate to reclaim both his occupied homeland and his stolen life.

But when in 1945 Poland was officially handed to the Soviets at the Yalta Conference, Michal knew there was nothing he could do to save his country. He needed a new life and a new plan, so he headed to London where determination saw him gain a degree in aeronautics and marry a well-bred 'English rose' – Mel's mother, Rosy.

The past wasn't buried while Mel was growing up, but it was rarely discussed either. 'Every weekend,' Mel recalled, 'other dads in the cul-de-sac would be out playing darts or mowing the lawn, but our dad would be inside researching his family.'

Because while Michal had found comfort in his new suburban lifestyle and growing family, he was still haunted by his turbulent early years and particularly by what had happened to his father. The weight of memory was strong, and led him to spend years researching and writing a book on his experiences – *The Crater's Edge* – which would finally be published in 2010.

Back in those early years, Michal tried not to let the lingering nightmares of his experiences affect his own children, who grew up with everything they could hope for. But children, especially intelligent sensitive ones like Mel, are often a lot more perceptive than they're given credit for. As a result, the Giedroyc clan learned a lot about gratitude, inner strength and how to find the determination to achieve great things.

'I think a lot of children of immigrant parents have a desire to prove themselves,' says Mel. 'He made a great life for himself in England out of nothing… You've got to make the most of everything because no one will do it for you.'

When Mel was 11, for example, her older brother Miko got her a job doing various forms of manual labour on a barge. 'I had to fell trees for wood, pull really dangerous nails out of the barge and just generally do what a 30-year-old man should have been doing,' she recalled in *The Guardian* in 2004. 'I was paid 20p an hour. It only went on for two weeks. I was really chuffed at the time. I probably blew it on a T-shirt and sweets, I should imagine. It was absolutely appalling.'

But it was characteristic of the Giedroycs that Mel didn't complain or give up at any point during those two weeks – because the family ethic was much stronger than that. The Giedroyc children were clearly also a keenly attentive bunch, and they had definitely listened to Michal when he told them one particular tale.

'They certainly remembered bits,' Michal explained in 2010 to the *Daily Express* to promote his book. 'When they were young we lived in leafy Surrey where we made friends with our neighbours and everyone was very nice.

'Then suddenly the neighbours became very cool and distant and when I confronted them I found out my children had been telling people that their father had been imprisoned. My neighbours thought I was a hardened criminal, and I had to do some damage limitation...'

To Mel and her siblings he was just a normal father, and her family just like any other family, but they were slowly picking up details about Michal's past. 'Dad must have told us things about his life when we were children but when you are young details don't really register,' she once explained.

It was at her first school, St Peter's Primary in Ashtead, Surrey, that Mel began her own journey – through academia. It was the 1970s, a notoriously difficult time to be in the British public education system, and Mel had to put up with being bullied mercilessly for being intelligent, well-behaved and eager to learn. She eventually found a way to cope: 'I spent the first four years being the apple of the teacher's eye and being bullied for it,' she told *The Independent* in 2009. 'Then from eight to eleven I found it easier to be the person wise-cracking at the back of the class.'

Mel's mum Rosy was an elegant and well-spoken woman, who wore bohemian headscarves when picking up her children from school. Mel was terrified of being called posh in front of her classmates and soon came up with an ingenious solution: 'I put on an estuary mockney accent and pretended I was adopted,' she said in the same interview with *The Independent*.

Mel told the newspaper that there were two sets of skinhead boys who ruled her class and spent all their time beating people up – 'one pair went straight to Borstal and then prison' – and they were largely left to carry on by the motley crew of teachers at the school, including a hardcore old-school Hattie Jacques-lookalike who wore brooches and 'scary traffic warden shoes', a bunch of woolly, hippy types and a random spattering of nuns.

Years later, she was asked by a fellow alumnus of St Peter's (a cameraman on the kids' show *Sorry, I've Got No Head*) how on earth she had survived it. But Mel recalls her time there fondly for the life-lessons it taught her, and credits *The Muppet Show* for helping her through the tougher moments of her schooldays. 'It got me through that sick feeling on Sunday nights about having to go in the next day,' she has said. 'It was hilarious and I was in love with Sam the Eagle.'

Mel's childhood nickname was 'Mrs Miggins', after the Pie Shop owner in *Blackadder*. She admits to being confused as to why her family gave her that particular pet name.

The first record she ever bought was Queen's 'Bohemian Rhapsody', which she played until it wore down; her first kiss was with a lad called Graham Francis at a Leatherhead church youth club disco in 1978; and her first obsession was with *Blue Peter* – she loved the show for years and never missed an episode. 'I even created the Leslie Judd Appreciation Society and charged my friends £2 to join,' she told the *Daily Record* in 1996. 'When I was 15, I met Leslie at an event in Oxford and told her about it. She was utterly bemused.'

And as with so many well-loved performers, it was Mel's first experience of a West End show that first started her down the theatrical road she is still travelling today. 'We saw *Peter Pan* and it was a life-changing moment,' she told the *Evening Standard* in 2013. Another big hint as to what was in store for Mel's future came when her brother introduced her to the subversive TV show *Not the Nine O'clock News*. She was entranced by it, as she told the *Evening Standard* in the same interview: 'I'll never forget Pamela Stephenson's incredible skit as Kate Bush singing in "My Leotard".'

But it was being bought tickets by her mum for a comedy

sketch show when she was 16 that best defines the memories of those early years – and marked the start of her own comedy career. Mel was going through an experimental phase at the time and had cut her hair into short spikes. She was obsessed with army surplus shops, so mainly wore monkey boots and baggy overalls, and had taken to plastering her face in pale foundation to mask the teenage T-bar of spots that had recently begun to grace her skin.

However, when she sat down with her sister and watched the live sketch show, certain things suddenly became clear: 'I remember sitting there,' she told *The Big Issue* in 2012, 'It was like the sun breaking through the clouds, a real road to Damascus moment, choirs in my head. I just thought, this is it, what I've been searching for. An incredible moment.'

It was also around that time that the Giedroyc family moved from Surrey to Oxford, and Mel swapped public school for private: she easily passed an entrance exam and began attending Oxford High School for Girls. In an interview with *The Independent* in 2009 she described how she still remembers the joy of walking into class on her first day and noticing that it was so quiet and 'everyone listened to the teachers'.

She relayed to the newspaper an anecdote from the time to illustrate the difference between the schools.

Once, in Religious Studies, the teacher asked: 'What do you think of when I say "God"?'

A girl replied: 'The Praying Hands by Albrecht Dürer.'

Mel recalled: 'I thought, "We're not in St Peter's anymore..."'

Oxford High School had an excellent Drama Department and Mel spent a lot of time writing plays. She would have acted in them too, but unfortunately she was plagued with repeated bouts of tonsillitis, which deprived her of her voice for some time.

Eventually the offending tonsils were removed, the operation coinciding with a rush of hormones that made Mel blossom into a woman almost overnight. She had always been a small, skinny child, who could eat anything and everything, and with her short hair she had been nicknamed 'Sonny' when she first arrived at the Oxford school.

'I looked like a boy, really,' she once told *The Mirror*. 'And family meals were key events, so we grew up loving food. I'd get home from school and hoof into a whole loaf of bread, an entire packet of biscuits.'

But after her much-needed op, the ultra-skinny 17-year-old really began to 'grow'. 'Boobs – the whole thing' she told *The Mirror*. 'All at once in this mad post-tonsil rush. I started to put on weight. From then on I had to be careful.'

Mel was a studious and intelligent child with a determination that saw her excel in most subjects but particularly English and foreign languages. She wasn't quite as proficient in maths and science: she was asked to stop doing physics when she illustrated an essay about a frozen river with all the ice on the bottom.

Gaining an impressive clutch of 'A' passes in her A Levels – in English, French and Italian – Mel applied for and got into Trinity College at Cambridge University. It was an incredible achievement and her family was rightly proud of their clever 'Mrs Miggins'.

'That was my peak,' she has since joked to *The Independent*: 'I got into Cambridge and it all went downhill. I did comedy and drink.' But it was also at that prestigious learning establishment that Mel would meet the person who was to become her lifelong friend and comedy partner, Sue Perkins.

CHAPTER 2

MEET SUE...

'I was always plagued with shyness. I still am.
I've just learnt to cover it up.'
Sue Perkins, *Woman & Home* magazine

She may act like Mel's more ironic and sardonic older sister, but Susan Elizabeth Perkins was actually born a year later than her comedy partner – on 22 September 1969, in East Dulwich, South London.

In contrast to 'baby of the family' Mel, Sue was the eldest child in the Perkins' household, but she felt a similar sense of awe at her siblings. Her younger sister, Michelle, was – as she once described in *Woman & Home* magazine – 'blonde and very girly and incredibly clever', while her younger brother David was 'big, burly and handsome'.

'I always felt like the thing made with the bit of plasticine that was left over,' she continued, somewhat more than humbly. From these few words it would be easy to make the assumption that Sue had a trying childhood, but in actual fact, the Perkins were – and still are – an incredibly close family.

On Mel and Sue's first official website, it jokingly said that she is the daughter of an Estonian beautician and one of Ken Dodd's 'Diddy Men', but in reality her early life was nowhere near as exotic: her hard-working dad, Bert, worked for a car dealership in Croydon, while her mother, Ann, was a secretary. And growing up in a cosy Surrey semi, Sue was a very happy child.

At school – first St Anne's Convent School, then Croham Hurst Independent School for Girls – she had a large and diverse gang of friends and was never bullied.

With her natural flair for humour and drama she fitted in with both the swots and the cool kids. She was however, extremely shy, a personality trait that she has now clearly learnt to control but she admits it will always be part of who she is.

'In certain situations shy people can access a different part of themselves,' she told *Woman & Home*. 'That's why when I'm at work I can bellow and gurn as I do but when I go home I am quiet and recessive. At heart I'm quite an awkward soul.'

As part of her shyness, Sue struggled with a stammer until she was around 13, and spent a lot of time in speech therapy – standing in the middle of cold rooms practising reading out loud. As she told *The Scotsman* in 2005: 'My fear was always that I couldn't communicate. When you have a stammer or a stutter it's just so frustrating because you have something in your head that you really want to communicate, a joke or a stupid saying or an observation, and you're just stuck in the middle of it.'

The stammer sometimes still returns when she's stressed or tired, but for the most part Sue communicates better than most people – through a dry, often crude humour, punctuated by a carefree silliness that belies the deeply thoughtful person she is on the inside.

Though she was universally liked at school, Sue was, as she puts it, a 'geeky' child. But it seems wrong to reiterate something so self-effacing. A better way of describing her early years would be that she was a sensitive and intelligent youngster, who was comfortable with her own company and loved to read and write.

As an adult, she says, she's not much different.

'I was a geeky child and I seem to have developed into a bigger version as an adult,' she revealed in the same 2005 *Scotsman* interview. 'I remain quite isolated. I'll either split my time being incredibly gregarious, talking to everyone and anyone, and then shutting it all down when I get home. I don't really have much of an in between.'

She felt trapped in her own head, which is why writing was so important to her. It was a way of turning herself inside-out on paper, getting everything that she usually struggled to communicate out into the open. It still is an important part of her life and work, indeed she says one of the proudest moments of her career so far was when her self-penned show *Heading Out* was commissioned by BBC2 and screened in 2013.

From the age of four, Sue wanted to be an eye surgeon. She'd had a squint and had to have an eye exam before a minor operation to correct it, and found the whole experience fascinating. 'I had to wear big glasses and have thick lenses slotted in,' she told *The Mirror* in 2005.

But that dream was never going to be reality: 'I failed every science and maths exam I ever took,' she added in the same interview, revealing another similarity to her pal Mel. 'I also realised I might have to touch eyes, which I'm squeamish about. And that I'd have to work hard. That put me off.'

In her teenage years Sue admits she was a bit of a rebel – cheeky and badly behaved – but she loved school. 'I was the remedial court jester, i.e. not funny,' she told *The Mirror*. One of her earliest memories is of kissing a boy called Anthony in front of a statue of The Virgin Mary, when she was about six. Mel has teased her about being such an early starter, telling interviewers that Sue once snogged 40 people at a party. 'It was actually 14,' admonished Sue at the time. 'But I liked snogging.'

The stories Sue tells of her early years growing up in the suburbs are largely unremarkable. She learnt piano to Grade 8 standard before giving it up as a teenager. Her first job, which she began aged 15, involved cleaning toilets at a local hotel. ('I remember one of the guests tipped me a bag of pistachio nuts for cleaning his toilet, which was quite mean, as he'd actually pebble-dashed quite badly.' *The Mirror*)

It wasn't glamorous but it paid £1.50 an hour, which was enough for Sue's essential weekly purchases – cigarettes, chewing gum, *Just 17* magazine and a pop single from Woolworths. And as compensation for the grubby job, while she worked she got to listen to the Radio 1 quiz shows that she so loved – and which she would be a guest on herself just a decade or so later.

While Sue was scrubbing porcelain, most of her friends worked at the local department store, Allders – including her first boyfriend, Richard. Sue first set eyes on Richard aged 17 during rehearsals for a school play. 'I looked at him from my raised promontory on a block in the gym hall and thought, "hunk"', she once revealed to the *Daily Mail*. I got a friend to tell him I fancied him.'

She used to sneak into the store and 'peek at him from behind the bath mats' (he worked in the bathroom fittings department), until eventually, she 'wore him down' and they began dating.

For those of you who are now confused – yes, Sue is a lesbian. But she didn't discover her feelings for women until she was in her mid-twenties. It was only much later that she would struggle so frantically with her fear of revealing her sexuality to the world.

She wasn't a closeted teenager, hiding her true self for the sake of normality; frightened of emotions she was feeling but didn't understand. She loved Richard deeply – they were together for more than six years and planned to spend the rest of their lives together.

'It was one of the best relationships I've had,' she told *The Daily Mail*, years later. 'We were even unofficially engaged. We went to Ratners [a now defunct mass-market jewellery store] and bought two rings: nine-carat gold. Bloody classy.'

Her teenage years were, therefore, typical of a girl growing up in Croydon. She went to school, before hanging out afterwards at the Royal Oak multi-storey car park with her friends, smoking and gossiping like every other teen.

She used to meet Richard at the halfway point between their two houses – a set of steps on Warren Road, where they'd sit and snog. 'Our parents thought we were spending too much time together so I'd say I was going out to get the papers.'

Drunken nights out would be at Croydon's finest nightclub, Cinderella's. She was never the type to dance round her handbag – Sue preferred indie music bands like The Clash and The Smiths, and was in love with Stewart Copeland from The Police.

She was no goody-two-shoes: unlike well-behaved Mel, she'd sometimes skive off school to go and have a smoke in the local park. It was partly because of this lax attitude to attendance that the teachers at her Catholic grammar school eventually declared that she wasn't 'university material'.

But instead of nodding in agreement and heading straight into the world of work, their words only made Sue determined to prove them wrong: almost in defiance, she won a place to read English Literature at Cambridge University, bringing her one step closer to meeting her comedy bestie, Mel.

But first she took a gap year, 10 months of which she filled by working in, of all places, the cookery department of a bookshop. It was the first hint to her future career, which would – quite accidentally – somehow always be associated with food.

From her first taste of Mel and Sue fame with *Light Lunch*, to her eating partnership with Giles Coren for *Supersizers*, followed by the revival of her old presenting friendship with Mel for *The Great British Bake-Off* – food has been as much the key to Sue's success as her dearest friend Mel.

CHAPTER 3

THE UNI YEARS

*'I remember meeting Sue. I think she thinks that we didn't
actually speak then, but I remember saying something to her.
Maybe she just ignored me, she probably did.'*
Mel Giedroyc, *The Independent,*

Because Sue was younger than Mel and took a gap year, the pair were in different year groups and moved in largely different circles during their time at Cambridge University.

While Sue was studying English literature at New Hall College, Mel was studying Italian language and literature at Trinity College – and both were enjoying the freedom of expression that being a university student offers. They cut their hair short and dyed it various colours, wore experimental Day-Glo clothes and partied. A lot. Mel had aspirations to tread the boards as a serious actress, while Sue was all about the writing side of things.

They both had typical university experiences. For example, as part of her degree course, Mel lived abroad for a year to teach English in Bologna, Italy. At the time she was a very heavy smoker and a big coffee-drinker and wasn't used to the early starts that teaching in the Italian education system entailed.

She didn't cope well. 'I got very, very thin, and then I got ill,' she has told *The Daily Mirror*. 'I had to give up smoking, give up coffee – had to just totally de-stress. And then I put on loads of weight. I had a moped, so I didn't do any exercise at all.'

It didn't help that she lived above an ice-cream shop and opposite a pizzeria, and as such she reached 12 stone before the year was over. When she got back home her mother was appalled and immediately put her on a healthy diet.

Cambridge is one of the most exclusive universities in the country and from the moment they arrived in that beautiful city the two women found themselves surrounded by students from the very heights of British society. But being suburban and middle class, it wasn't what either of them were used to, and as a result they weren't entirely comfortable – especially Mel.

'At Trinity College there was a coterie of the poshest of the posh, people you didn't ever see, they were so posh,' Mel said in a 2009 interview with *The Independent*. 'They went to each other's rooms and, at weekends, each other's estates. I preferred to be with the weirdo bunch of raggle-taggle thesps.'

She found the 'raggle-taggle' thesps at the university's Footlights Comedy Club, and, after passing the audition process, joined immediately. Founded in 1883, the Cambridge University Footlights Dramatic Club – commonly referred to simply as the Footlights – has been run by university students ever since. For decades it has dominated the British world of comedy – spawning groups such as the Monty Python members and The Goodies.

A large number of its former members have gone on to win Baftas, Oscars and countless other awards, and have enjoyed long and successful careers in the entertainment and media industry.

Today, Footlights is seen as an unofficial finishing school for many of Britain's most well-known comics and entertainers. Cast-members have included Morwenna Banks, Clive Anderson, David Baddiel, Alexander Armstrong and David Armand. It was the perfect place for Mel and Sue to meet and get to know each other and, most importantly, to practice their trade.

In 1988, Mel had just come back to Cambridge after the summer holidays, which she had mainly spent on a beach in the Mediterranean. Wearing a variety of rave gear, including a boiler suit, bandana and a whistle, she attended a Footlights comedy evening commonly known as a 'smoker'. Made up of roughly 20 three-minute sketches, songs or stand-up routines, it was a chance for Footlights newbies to practise performing their original material in front of the Footlights committee.

One of those newbies was a skinny, tall, spiky raven-haired girl called Sue Perkins, who was performing because she had lost a bet with a friend and was woefully under-prepared.

For Mel, who was in the audience watching, Sue's performance was a revelation. Not only was she female, unlike most of the students there, but she was incredibly, effortlessly funny. Sue says she was terrified: 'I was like a Christian being thrown to the lions. I chain-smoked my way through it,' she described to *Time Out*.

But although Sue is convinced it went badly wrong, Mel disagrees, as she stated in *The Independent* in 1999, at the height of their first time success. 'That night there was a dreadful guy who came up on stage to do a gag about confusing Pyrex with Durex, all about going out with this hot dish,' she recalled, continuing: 'There was a slightly tumbleweed atmosphere in that cellar – beer, carpets, smoke. Suddenly out of nowhere came this mad, six-stone pixie figure. She leapt on to the stage, and it was Perks. She looked like an alarmed rooster, her hair a cockscomb.

She had three fags on the go, and obviously had no material. She just grabbed the mike and did this ramble for 15 minutes, and brought the house down.

'I went up to her and said something very cheesy like, "Hello Sue, welcome to the bosom of comedy. Would you like to do some gags?"'

It was a very Mel thing to do – a friendly welcoming gesture, but Sue was so overwhelmed by the whole stand- up experience that the meeting is a little more fuzzy in her memory than Mel's.

'Mel likes to think of herself as a Svengali figure,' she half-joked in the same interview. 'She hung around like an impresario trying to be a big fish in the tiny Cambridge pond. There is a vague memory of someone in Day-Glo clothes, bleach-blonde hair and fake tan, which in retrospect must have been Mel. I don't know anyone else who would go around looking like that.'

Mel invited Sue to her birthday party, which took place three weeks later, and it was there that the two properly met – and instantly bonded. Well, sort of. 'I remember meeting her properly three weeks later, on her birthday, in a club,' she said in the *Independent* interview. 'Club is too posh a title – in a pit with wall-to-wall smoked glass and cork tiles on the ceiling, a smell of dead rodents.'

When she found her, Mel was '… totally off her face. Flecks of vomit were around her mouth, and she was doing really bad early house dancing, flailing arms knocking everyone over. She called me Barbara, Sheila, Debbie – didn't have a clue who I was.' (*The Independent*.)

It kick-started a series of evenings where Sue would go out and watch Mel get hideously, outrageously drunk and the two became mates. 'You would be able to work out where Mel was by following her stomach contents, the piles of puke,' she said in the 1999 *Independent* interview. 'She would fall asleep while everyone around her cleared up.'

The duo got on extremely well, both being from similar family backgrounds and obsessed with the city of London. Having grown up just outside of the metropolis in matching '*Terry and June*-style surburbias', they were both desperate to move to the 'big smoke' and live what they perceived to be a cool London lifestyle. They laughed at the same things, didn't take things too seriously and felt comfortable with each other from the very beginning.

And although they didn't know it at the time, the 'fooling around with making people laugh' that they amused themselves with, would keep them together for decades to come.

Mel and Sue joined up with two guys – there were far more men than women in the Footlights – and began performing sketches, with Sue acting as compère. But while Mel was using the experience as practice for what she saw as her future serious acting career, Sue didn't see it as anything of the sort. To her, it was just a bit of fun.

'I never viewed stand-up as a career option,' she has said. 'I wanted to write – I saw comedy as part of my social life. I think women are less likely to view it as a job.'

After just a few months of comedy experience, which included their first taste of heckling (Mel was told she had chubby knees on stage), they travelled to Edinburgh with a group of Footlights members to perform at the Fringe Festival, a mainstay of the comedy calendar for anyone who has designs on being a stand-up comic.

It was there that they met someone else who would become

very important to both the women: Emma Kennedy. Now an award-winning comedian, author, scriptwriter and actor, back then Emma was performing with the Footlights' mortal enemies – The Oxford Revue. Standing on stage with fellow comedian Richard Herring, she couldn't help but stare when Herring whispered darkly, *'that's the fucking Cambridge Footlights...'*

Emma spotted a blonde in pink dungarees 'with ludicrous 1980s hair and sensational teeth that looked as if they should have their own gravitational pull', and couldn't help but laugh at the girl she would later be introduced to as Mel. They shouldn't have become friends, but they did. 'It was the Jets and the Sharks,' was how Emma described the situation, in an interview years later.

Emma and Mel were set to be firm friends – they are still in touch to this day – even if Mel had to get over a little bit of jealousy first. 'She was absolutely hilarious and compelling to watch,' she has recalled. 'We got chatting afterwards and I remember thinking, "Oh my God, she's so funny – and very pretty". But although it was Mel who first made friends with Emma, many years later it would be Sue who she would be closest to, because they eventually became a couple.

Back in Cambridge, Mel and Sue continued their studies, without any inkling of starting a career together. Sue became the well-respected president of the Footlights Society, while Mel did radical theatre, 'which meant wearing urine-coloured pyjamas and shaving my head'.

Mel got a 2:2 in her finals, after writing her final essay on *Monty Python*. 'I hadn't written an essay in Italian during the four-year course, so I put together a massive amount of information, put it on a tape and learned it by heart.'

Sue graduated with a degree in English literature and a bad

taste in her mouth from the experience. After scrutinising authors and writing for three intense years, she found it hard to enjoy the simple pleasure of reading again. 'It killed it for me,' she bluntly told *The Guardian* in 2006.

It was a problem she would struggle with for a number of years and would not bode well for the writing career she'd previously had her heart set on. But it was good news for everyone else, because comedy was so far removed from the work she had been studying, Sue now turned to it in earnest.

Both women graduated in 1990, and neither had the faintest idea what they would do next.

CHAPTER 4

DREAMS AND HARD GRAFT

*'All the bad gigs merge into one grey, rainy van trip around these
sceptred isles that seems to have lasted seven fucking years.'*
Mel Giedroyc, *Metro*, 2012.

Leaving university and heading out into the real world is undoubtedly a culture shock. And after leaving the cocoon of comedy in which they were living, Mel and Sue were unprepared for the confusion that groping their way through their twenties would entail. It would be seven years before they got their first big break – nearly a decade of being broke, feeling desperate and rejected.

'If I was starting out now, I probably wouldn't do it,' Mel told a *Guardian* journalist for an interview in 2003. 'But when you're young and hungry and you haven't got responsibilities you can do anything if you set your mind to it.'

Mel still had her heart set on being a serious actress and began auditioning for various drama schools. None of them accepted her, which she put down to her 'cavalier attitude' of breezing in and out of auditions.

Meanwhile, Sue was having a similar crisis of confidence. 'When I was young I wanted to be the female Dostoyevsky until I realised that I wasn't very talented,' she later recalled to *The Independent*. Instead she had sort of decided to be a teacher, or possibly a lecturer.

But, as she added in the interview: 'It was only after we left university that I realised I wasn't going to have a responsible job.'

Mel probably would have continued auditioning for drama school places, and in all likelihood been successful, if tragedy hadn't struck and changed the course of her life and, indirectly, Sue's.

Soon after Mel graduated, her mum Rosy suffered a near-fatal stroke. 'It was just when I'd left university,' she told the *Daily Mail* in 2013. 'It was really scary – terrifying. We were just literally living hour-by-hour. She was on the point of checking out and saying some pretty final things to us, like, "stay close to each other". You know the kind of thing.'

Mel's life was instantly put on hold as she prayed for her mum to survive. Amazingly, Rosy did indeed begin to pull through and was eventually allowed home to recover. But the recovery process itself was long and slow and Mel made the decision to stay at home and devote herself to looking after her bedridden mother. She would remain there for nearly a year.

Drama school was now completely out of the question, but as she busied herself tidying the house and entertaining and caring for Rosy, she suddenly had an idea. She sat down and wrote a letter to Sue, who received it 'in the midst of the failure of my writing career'. Sue was struggling with her own future at the time and beginning to wonder if she'd ever find her own niche.

'*Dear Sue,*' she wrote, '*I have been thinking – would you like to come and form a double act with me? Would you like to? Do let me know. Love Melanie.*'

Sue still has the letter – it is a reminder of the humility behind their beginnings, of how far they've come together, and of their most desperate times.

'We had nothing else we could do, for God's sake,' Mel eventually explained to *The Independent* in 2009. Sue agreed pretty much instantly. Together they began to write sketches and jokes, and practise performing them together.

They began writing for Radio 4's *Weekending* once a week, and received £8 per line for their gags. 'You'd go into a room with 40 other people, just for the warmth and free BBC coffee,' Mel has said.

'I would write these enormous great diatribes,' Sue said in the same *Independent* interview. 'I wrote a three-parter once, absolutely terrible, but they put it on and we got about £150. I don't think any money I earned subsequently ever felt as good. At the time that was huge.' Huge, but not huge enough to live off…

During the election in 1992 the duo decided to moon out of the window at John Major. 'We thought we were so left-wing,' Sue recalled in an interview years later with blogger Mary Comerford (http://freespace.virgin.net/mad.yak/HTML/Mel_and_Sue/interviews.htm). 'But when we saw him we just waved like children. Our big political statement went out the window and it was a case of: "You're on the telly! You're John Major!"'

As the months passed, it was clear they needed regular money to survive. They would both have to get regular work to supplement their comedy careers.

A year later they each had jobs, were sleeping on friends' floors and were gigging regularly all over the country in terrible venues. While Rosy was getting better, Mel still did her cleaning for a small wage, as well as working as a barmaid at the Jongleurs comedy club in London and sometimes doing telesales shifts.

It was an erratic life, but she was happy and felt very lucky that her brother Miko had a spare room she could sometimes stay in. She was working hard for a pittance and gigging in car parks and churches, but she still managed to fit in a bit of acting too. She set up a little theatre company with fellow Cambridge graduates Stephen Mangan (now a household name thanks to dark comedy *Green Wing*) and James Harding (now Head of BBC News) and spent lots of time at Mangan's flat in Chalk Farm, North London.

'The flat was usually full of actors talking well into the night about drama and putting the world to rights,' Mangan told *The Sunday Times* in 2009. 'I have a horrible feeling that we were quite noisy; we were all speaking from our diaphragms and projecting, because at the time we were having our voices trained so that we could be heard at the back of a large theatre. We'd rehearse plays in the flat before we performed above a pub in Camden.'

Sue was equally busy trying to drum up enough cash to live off. Her first 'proper' job was teaching drama at a girl's comprehensive school in North London. 'One play took us three months to rehearse,' she told the *Sunday Mirror* in 2005. 'On the first night the girls asked if they could do something to relax before the show. I agreed and to my astonishment they all started smoking dope. I left after that.'

Her brief stint as a teacher was followed by a string of temping jobs. 'I manned the phones for a financial publishing house, but after a week I said I had Pollution Hay Fever, which meant I couldn't work in London," she said in the same interview. 'But my Pollution Hay Fever didn't stop me signing-on.'

Next she sold carpet cleaner door-to-door and tried her hand at copywriting, but struggled to sound convincing because she thought the products were all useless. She, like Mel, also borrowed money heavily from various banks and family members.

Then, in the summer of 1993, the very novice duo decided they fancied having another go at performing at the Edinburgh Fringe Festival, just as it was about to start.

The Festival is the largest arts festival in the world. If you can make it there, as the phrase goes, you can make it anywhere. Nowhere else has such a wide variety of performances available for audiences to see at any one time, and as such, it is a theatre- and comedy-lover's dream.

Anyone who has been will know that the array of acts available day and night is almost overwhelming. Besides all the shows that are being put on in the mainstream venues, it is impossible to walk down the Edinburgh streets without constantly stumbling across impromptu performances and having flyers thrust at you promoting gigs in smaller venues, pubs and upstairs rooms.

It offers a cornucopia of talent, an excess of entertainment and more laughs, drama or experimentation than would be available on any TV channel for probably an entire year.

These days, the figures are incredible. In 2013, there were 45,464 performances of 2,871 shows. An estimated 24,107 performers took part and a record-breaking 1,943,493 tickets were issued for shows, events and exhibitions in 273 venues across the city. And these numbers don't include the tens of thousands attending the hundreds of free, non-ticketed events at the Fringe, from tented comedy to street theatre.

For most actors and performers it is an annual event where they have the chance to meet up with or just observe former fellow cast members, rivals, or friends performing their latest work – or just in passing in the street.

For comedians, Edinburgh has become a critical repeat destination on their road map to success. There is not a single comedian working on television today who has not at some point appeared at the Edinburgh Fringe. Most regard it as the pinnacle of their year, the point around which they anchor new material, and the springboard from which to launch new tours.

In 1993, Mel and Sue had absolutely no idea what they were doing, or any semblance of a plan – but they did have a friend who worked at C Venue on Princes Street in Edinburgh, at a relatively new performing space that had only been open for a year.

The only slot he had left for them was at 10am – not a typical or popular time for anyone but the most hardened festival-goers to attend. They took it, and 'The Naked Brunch' was born.

The experience was both uplifting and disheartening. 'For three and a half weeks we were getting up at 8am and trotting off to a venue where we usually represented double our audience,' Sue recalled to *The Metro* in 2009. 'I remember one woman who didn't even take her rucksack off. She sat at a very strange angle, leaning forward with this huge bag on her back, our sole audience.'

But there was something about starting out that enthralled the duo, and they soaked up this new experience of regular gigs, late nights and hope like a sponge.

Sue later told Scottish newspaper the *Daily Record*: 'Don't get me started on the joys of a spicy haggis in the middle of the night on Lothian Road, sitting on the pavement amidst the dog poo…'

Although their average audience was one person, they loved

every minute of their first proper Fringe experience. 'We let loose our double act with all the impact and artistic savagery of a Rosie and Jim Roadshow,' Mel told *The Sunday Times* a few years later.

And half way through their Fringe run they were astonished to discover that *The Times* had picked their act at random to write about, which boosted their profile and put bums on their seats for the rest of the festival.

They did have a unique selling point: 'Back in 1993, when we started, we were pretty much the only female double act on the scene,' Mel has said. The only other notable female duo was the mega-famous French and Saunders, so there was a definite gap for them in the market. Mel and Sue dreamed of reaching their kind of stellar heights, especially when, at the end of their first Fringe run, they were nominated for the prestigious Fringe Newcomer of the Year Award, which had a history of being somewhat of a kingmaker in the comedy world.

But they didn't win – hitting the big time was not to be that simple for Mel and Sue. 'It gave us the illusion of success, but then we had nothing for years and survived by temping and borrowing,' Sue told *The Independent*, seven years later.

They headed back to London, and consequently to a life of hard comedy graft, slogging away, waiting for their next big break. For the next four years life was unstable, exciting and exhausting. 'Sue and I had a week once where we lived off luncheon vouchers while travelling on rail vouchers,' Mel recalled in the same interview.

They took their double act of sketches and stand-up to a string of arts centres and small venues around the country, but were never really on the main comedy circuit – they say it's because they were 'never cool enough'.

However, after *The Times* had championed them, people had

started to take notice of the duo and a certain amount of hype preceded them wherever they went. It made them nervous, as they didn't feel they could live up to it – instead it felt like the critics were ready to tear them apart at every gig they did. Eventually the hype died down, leaving them back to where they started, which was right at the bottom of the comedy pile.

They did the Edinburgh Fringe Festival every year, and on their second residency in 1994, Sue bumped into Emma Kennedy on a night out. As Emma recalled in an interview with *The Independent* in 2008: 'We went off and got plastered and at the end of the evening she said, "Why don't you come and stay with me and Mel?" That was it. They became my best friends.'

Emma had trained as a lawyer after university but was in the process of giving it up to be a comedian, so she began script editing for the duo. It led to some fun times. Emma recounted one of these moments in the same interview with *The Independent*, prefacing it by saying that the three of them were the 'squarest people in show business'. (If that's true, then they've certainly made it hip to be a square.)

'The wildest time I've ever had with Mel was when we somehow ended up going to Amsterdam with a member of KLF. I had never up to this point had a drug in my life. We were taken to a hotel and this huge marijuana joint gets passed around. I take two puffs and next thing I know I'm in the foetal position on the floor, rocking and shouting, "I'm having a bad trip".

'Mel is totally off her face, and I think Sue is a giant with no head who's come to kill me, so I try to punch her. Eventually, Mel realised I was in trouble and gave me a cup of coffee.' Luckily they all survived the experience.

By 1995, Mel and Sue were still touring around the country, staying in terrible B&Bs and getting nowhere. They hit a particularly low point in Leighton Buzzard when they did a show that went so badly they had to leave the theatre via the back exit. Then, in Stockton-on-Tees they went on stage after a very heavy lecture about domestic abuse and absolutely bombed.

'We came on full of energy doing *Brown Owl* characters and the audience looked absolutely devastated,' Mel later recounted to the *Metro*. 'That was a very poor booking. We had no idea what was going on. We then attended an all-women disco with both victims and perpetrators of domestic abuse. We had to bop around to "We Are Family".'

But at the Fringe that summer, they made a bit of a breakthrough: their 'Women in Uniform' gigs were a sell-out and without the hype that had made them so nervous before, they absolutely stole the show.

The Independent was impressed: 'Unlike the rest of this year's successful female acts, their made-for-TV show is sketch-based and non sex-oriented,' read the newspaper's review. 'Instead of targeting men, they dish it out to Emma Thompson and give a masterful impression of Liz Hurley trying to act her way out of a paper bag.'

They were subsequently asked by the team behind *The Little Picture Show* to do some work for the ITV film review programme, which was presented by Mariella Frostrup. They jumped at the chance, and played characters called Marsha and Barsha, but again it wasn't enough to live off.

By now both Mel and Sue had moved into their own flat-shares, and rent money was becoming increasingly hard to come by. Sue was living with Emma Kennedy, the actress Nicola Walker, and writer Sarah Phelps, in a place that Walker described at the time as being a cross between a *Wayne's World* for women and *Girls Behaving Badly*.

'I love the people I live with,' Walker told *The Mirror* in 1998. 'When I open the front door there's usually at least one of them with a big bottle of wine just waiting to be drunk. Not that it's always harmonious. We're always arguing – real no-holds barred, chair-throwing, cursing and swearing episodes.'

Though they'd brushed up against the very edges of success early on in their careers, behind the scenes Mel and Sue were struggling, and the gigs weren't going down any better than they had when they'd started.

Times were tough, but, 'we stuck it out,' Sue said in an interview with *The Independent*. 'There were times when it was really difficult to know where your rent cheque was coming from. We had been educated, and it seemed pointless just pissing our life away. It's very hard to know when it's time to stop dreaming.'

And sometimes, no matter how well they got on, working so closely together would leave them grumpy and snarky with each other. But as bad as things were getting, the duo would have to reach real rock bottom before they could begin their incredible climb to the top.

CHAPTER 5

ROCK BOTTOM AND REVELATIONS

'The truth dawned late, I guess. And it came as
a thunderous shock.'
Sue Perkins, *Daily Mail*, 2013

B oth Mel and Sue were watching their twenties go past in a blur of poorly-paid gigs, cheap food and ever-decreasing hope. As they passed the midway mark and headed towards the landmark age of 30, their views on life began to change. And as they were still living their lives almost exactly as they had in their (now long-gone) university days, it must have been easy to feel as if they hadn't achieved very much at all.

Both women started to grapple with previously unfelt emotions. Mel began to get intensely broody: her older brother and sisters were all having children and she adored being an aunty. But although she had been dating – including a few passionate months with *Father Ted* writer Arthur Mathews – nothing had worked out and she began to panic that she'd never become a mother.

It affected her badly and made her angsty and sad, feelings that weren't being helped by the fact that she constantly had no money and was living a very transient lifestyle. Mel wanted stability and a family and it didn't look like either was going to happen any time soon.

But as difficult a time as Mel was having, Sue was finding dealing with her emotions twice as hard. Because she'd begun to have feelings she didn't recognise at all – feelings about women. Sue had always considered herself securely heterosexual. It hadn't even crossed her mind that she could have feelings for females; she had never experienced the pain and bewilderment of a confused identity and neither had she ever had to pretend to be attracted to men – to herself or others.

She'd dated her first love, Richard, for years and she'd had several boyfriends since their split. But then, triggering a flood of wildly disorienting emotions, a turbulent new passion moved her.

'I just fell in love with this woman,' she recalled to the *Daily Mail* in 2005. 'It was a terrible crush – not a sexual relationship at all, just a very charged platonic one. I remember feeling so miserable and so alive at the same time. It was like a second adolescence. I couldn't rest. I was in tumult: it was thrilling but there was total panic. I realised at that point that it was an emotional and spiritual connection – rather than a sexual one – that I lacked with men.'

Sue didn't have a bad experience with men that subsequently pushed her into the arms of women; in fact she finds it easier to be around men now that there is no sexual tension with them.

She told the same newspaper: 'Men are beautiful things, to be admired and adored – it's more widely recognised now that gay women are not man-hating separatists – but I just felt more comfortable with women.'

The revelation upended Sue's world, and in her words, really took her apart. 'Sexuality is so primal,' she told the *Daily Mail*. 'I had thought my life was safe and organised, and all of a sudden I was knocked for six. Among all the pain and weirdness, it was also very exciting and life-affirming. It was like chancing upon a secret.'

But it was a secret that would remain undisclosed from the rest of the world for some years yet. Sue began dating women and slowly took her tentative first few steps into what was, for her, an undiscovered world. And then, at around this confusing and exciting time, came another shock – in the form of an unusual answering machine message.

Dawn French and Jennifer Saunders, at that point at the pinnacle of their careers, were the only successful female double act around at the time, and had broken numerous comedy boundaries to get there. Their eponymous show had started in 1987 as a humble spoof sketch show, but immediately found its own niche and quickly grew in popularity as the eighties turned into the nineties.

The duo had taken large steps to dispel the myth that women couldn't be funny, and didn't rely on man-hating or crude humour to illicit a few cheap laughs.

Their work was observational and intelligent, appealed to a wide audience and quickly cemented a place for them at the top of the British comedy scene.

With bigger BBC budgets as the successful show's seasons passed, they were forever looking to champion new female talent, and when they first heard about Mel and Sue they were intrigued about their new female rivals. So they called them to offer them work.

'We thought it was someone taking the piss,' Mel later

explained to *The Mirror*, about hearing the answerphone message they had left. '"Hello, it's Jennifer Saunders, my number is da-da-da…" We went: "Yeah, yeah, yeah, right." But rang. We were completely bowled over when it was her.'

With much excitement, Mel and Sue began to write for the *French and Saunders* show, and even appeared in four episodes of it in 1996: 'Dr Quimn, Mad Woman', 'The Quick and the Dead', 'Franco e Sandro' and 'Loveheart'.

Their work was impressive, and the more seasoned comics immediately took them under their wing, seeing them as possibly the right pair to take over their mantle if and when they retired.

Things may not have worked out quite as French and Saunders envisioned, and in fact Mel and Sue's route to fame together would take an altogether much more circuitous route, and end up in a very different place. But the older duo have supported Mel and Sue from that first phone call right up to the present day, sending them congratulatory cards and going to see their shows and plays, or watching them on TV as and when they appeared.

'They're like that, though,' says Mel. 'Just very on-side.'

And although Mel and Sue were flattered when the comparisons with them began to inevitably occur, they believed it was only because they were another female double act. In actual fact they thought the foursome were very different – both in the characters they invented and the relationship they had with each other.

And as exciting as it was to work with the two queens of comedy, their money problems weren't getting solved, and the pair were growing deeper into debt. They picked up a few other bits of TV work as a result of their work on *French and Saunders*, but nothing life-changing.

In 1996, Mel and Sue played various roles, including a woman with an imaginary friend on *Fist of Fun* – a radio show turned TV series written by comedians Lee and Herring, with whom they were good friends.

They also starred uncredited as 'girls at birthday party' in the third episode of the Lloyds Bank Channel 4 Film Challenge (a series of short films made by winners of a competition) as well as being billed as 'Wife' (Sue) and 'Sister Mary' (Mel) in Episode 2 of *The Friday Night Armistice*. Their voices also made a disembodied appearance on comedy series *The Boss*, as radio show hosts/callers.

Mel, being an actress by trade, bagged herself a few more on-screen moments, playing various roles on *Never Mind the Horrocks*, and Mary Tinker in 'The Christmas Lunch Incident' episode of Dawn French's hit show *The Vicar of Dibley*.

But none of it was enough to live off. And what made it worse was that their TV exposure, although small and brief, only added to the hype that was now once more building up around them, and which they still didn't feel they were quite living up to.

They were working with such pros as Jane Horrocks, Jim Broadbent and of course, French and Saunders, but it wasn't translating into success for the duo. Something wasn't quite working and they couldn't figure out what. Was this as good as they were going to get?

That year, they had what Sue later described in Scotland's *Sunday Mail* as a particularly bad year at the Fringe: 'We had done our shows and really enjoyed them but we were over-hyped – far beyond our abilities,' she recalled. 'We never thought we were the next big thing but that's how we got touted. There was a big backlash and it was painful. We took a pasting. It felt like we were naughty kids being skelped on the backside.

She added in the interview: 'the thing about the festival is if you are having a bad time you will know about it. You walk into the Pleasance Courtyard and there is always a bitter performer doing a radical interpretation of the Bible, which nobody is coming to see who will ram a bad review into your face.'

Their new show, *Planet Pussycat*, was a whirlwind of crushed plum velvet and patchwork denim costumes, which prompted one reviewer to write: 'Cross Barbarella with French and Saunders and what do you get? Space skunks from Surrey.'

While the rest of that year's Fringe performers were clad in the obligatory uniform of black leggings, Mel and Sue were determined to be different. 'I think a lot of people are a bit fazed that we get all done up in these panto suits,' Mel told a reporter from *The Daily Record* at the time.

'But they really make us get up there and do it. We're not the kind of comedians who would stand up in tight black leggings and smoke fags and be cool. And the costumes are handy, because we use a lot of little props and we can keep them in the pockets.'

They told the newspaper that they really wanted the show to be fun – not acerbic, or sharp, or darkly witty, but proper belly-laughingly fun. 'We want the audience to know we're having the best time we could possibly have,' Sue told *The Daily Record*. 'It's like having a party – you've got to make an effort.' Mel tentatively added: 'They're not the funniest thing about us. There are the jokes as well.'

During the show, they made the most out of coming from Surrey and speaking the Queen's English, sending themselves up for the audience. Sue jokingly explained in the same interview with the *Daily Record*: 'It's a case of taking the mickey before someone else does. It doesn't take long to realise we don't have cool accents.'

The Fringe audiences got to meet a variety of Mel and Sue characters, including the swing beat duo 'VPL', the world's worst B&B owners Sinister Jan and Jim Seaspray, Daisy and Miranda, a pair of hippy chicks from the sixties, and many more.

But the reviews were mixed and the heckles were loud, and while they had initially enjoyed performing the show, the comedy pals felt thoroughly dejected by the time it was all over at the end of August.

As Sue recalled to the *Sunday Mail* a few years later: 'That was the year where we realised we were going to have to work at it rather than just coast on our luck which, to an extent, we had been doing.'

As 1996 turned into 1997, both Mel and Sue were tired of the endless road trips and crummy B&Bs, getting ripped off, gigs going wrong and the general feeling of treading water that they knew so well.

'It got you energised,' Mel said in the same interview, with more than a whiff of nostalgia. 'It kept you feeling young. But you can't deal with that stress for too long.'

Mel had reached her limit and wanted to give up. She went to visit Sue at her flat and told her that she just couldn't go on anymore. After seven years together the pair had hit rock bottom and both felt like failures.

They knew they were funny, and had faith that their material was good: but by now they were in their late twenties, they simply weren't making enough to survive on, and they knew that they couldn't keep up the lifestyle they were living, forever.

Mel owed around £9,000 and Sue owed more – £11,000. The pair discussed running a business together; talked about maybe opening a sandwich shop. But then, just as they were ready to throw in the towel for good, a surprising fax came through from their agent.

It was an invite to do a screen test for a brand new daily daytime show for Channel 4 called *Light Lunch*. At first, neither Mel nor Sue were keen to audition. They might have been desperate for work, but it was a cookery show, not the type of thing they had ever considered before, and it didn't seem like something they'd enjoy at all.

Also, if they were being completely honest with themselves, they'd probably have admitted that they were downhearted about their careers in general and had subconsciously started not to care anymore. But their agent forced them to do it, and so when the day of the screen test came, almost in defiance they completely ignored the script, messed around – and absolutely nailed it.

CHAPTER 6

LIGHT LUNCH

*'We'd go out there and wing it and were at our best
when Mel was cocking up and I was correcting her. We would
just gibber on, entertaining ourselves, basically.'*
Sue Perkins, *The Daily Telegraph*, 2006

It was almost too much to take in: after years of scraping by and repeated setbacks, Mel and Sue had their very own TV show. Granted, it was a lunchtime slot and not prime time, but it was theirs and would at last introduce them to a broad audience.

They had a real chance of becoming household names and it would all start now.

Their first contract was just for two weeks to test out the complete TV unknowns, but once they passed muster and signed contracts, the two women had money, stability and the beginning of a bright career.

It had all finally happened – just when they were about to give up. Fate certainly had a funny way of making people suffer for their success, but both Mel and Sue were now re-energised and ready, finally, to start their careers for real.

Princess Productions, a newly formed production company,

was put in charge of what was to be the initial, 60-episode run of *Light Lunch*, which began airing in March 1997.

The difficult to fill 12:30pm slot was a challenge for the team behind the show, which consisted of Princess's elegant co-founder Henrietta Conrad and her business partner Sebastian Scott, the nineties telly whiz-kid who was partially behind the success of *The Big Breakfast*, along with David Baddiel's brother Ivor who came on board as a comedy writer, and other staff who were recruited from the likes of *TFI Friday*, *The Big Breakfast* and even *Blue Peter*.

It was Scott and Conrad who had spotted Mel and Sue's potential at the screen test and signed them up to front the show. It would quickly prove to be an inspired decision for everyone involved.

Filmed in Studio 3 at The London Studios, Waterloo, in central London, the set was small but bright and cosy and perfect for the format. In fact, it was designed so well that it made the tiny area look liked a packed Wembley Stadium when the cameras started rolling.

Structured around making and eating lunch, Mel and Sue would chat to a guest chef while they made the meal, and then eat it accompanied by different celebrity guests who they then interviewed. Another guest would usually bring in dessert, and they'd all move to the settee for another chat and a couple of phone-in questions from viewers.

The whole thing was filmed live and lasted an hour and the studio audience brought in their own lunch to eat during the show. They were given a few quid each to cover the cost and the most unusual creations would be shown on camera. The show even had a house band, who were collectively known by various different food pun names, and would entertain the audience during breaks.

For the first two weeks, as with any new programme, hardly anyone tuned in. 'They had to phone round women's lunch clubs and anyone who would come in off the street for the audience,' Mel recalled in an interview with *The Scotsman* a few years later.

'And the faxes and calls on the phone-in were fakes too,' Sue added in the same 1998 interview. 'You'd get someone obviously from London pretending to be from Cornwall and wanting to talk to Mark Lamarr and we'd know it was Drew from the office. When we first got real people calling, we thought, how bizarre, there are real people watching.'

As the weeks passed and word travelled about the hip new show that everyone was missing out on, more and more people tuned in and Mel and Sue settled into a fine work rhythm.

The show became a cult classic in record time: housewives, students, slackers, pensioners – even prisoners – were all tuning in to see the energetic duo banter with their guests and eat lunch with their audience.

It wasn't polished. It wasn't perfectly scripted. But the years they'd spent honing their skills together immediately shone through and the duo worked so well together that their infectious giggles made them instantly popular. It quickly became apparent that Mel and Sue had something very different, something that people genuinely liked.

They each fell naturally into their own roles – Mel the ditzy pigtail-wearing blonde and Sue the darker more self-deprecating 'big sister', the sharper, more acerbic side of the duo.

Watching them ad-lib and riff off each other at lightning speed breathed new life into the previously stagnant lunchtime television slot, and made an otherwise formulaic show compulsive viewing.

Sandwiched between long-running children's show *Sesame Street* and a dull sea-life documentary, it fast became the rose between two thorns – the lunchtime boost of energy that British TV so badly needed.

That first season saw the duo entertain guests such as Richard Curtis, Ant and Dec, Johnny Vaughn, Kylie Minogue and even long-haired superstar crooner Michael Bolton. They affectionately teased and cajoled their guests, most of whom took it in good humour. They once did a *Star Wars*-themed episode and got Dave Prowse, the actor who controversially played Darth Vader but didn't voice him (Vader's deep, breathy voice was actually the husky tones of James Earl Jones) to appear in a sketch.

Considering that the matter of the disconnect between Darth Vader's voice, physical form and face (when his mask was taken off in *Return of the Jedi*, it was actor Sebastian Shaw who was underneath) had apparently been the subject of much tension, it was impressive that Mel and Sue had convinced him to say in his natural West Country accent: 'I can't understand why my voice didn't make the final cut...'

But you can't please everyone: Janet Street Porter and master chef Jean Christophe Novelli both got huffy when they failed to see the funny side of Mel and Sue's mockery, while the late great Kate O'Mara was very frosty with the duo during her interview.

O'Mara was appearing with her *Dynasty* co-star Stephanie Beacham, and Mel and Sue decided that they would make them feel at home by wearing eighties outfits – and doing a sketch poking fun at the popularly decadent drama.

'We had costumes and our hair done and brilliant make-up,' Mel later recalled to *Metro*. 'They were both in the Green Room watching and apparently it didn't go down well. Then they came on and we had to interview them. To say there was a certain amount of hostility coming off them would be an understatement. I'd researched Kate O'Mara's life and I was asking her questions and she said "No… no… no… that didn't happen." We were still in the costumes.'

But even when things went wrong, the audience still howled with laughter and the comedy pair's popularity quickly soared.

Mel and Sue both worked-off their debt and soon had made enough money to really start enjoying life again – Sue even put down a deposit on a three-bedroom house in Cricklewood, North London, and bought it for £190,000.

But there were downsides to their success too. The show was based around food, and eating delicious lunches every day made both women put on a considerable amount of weight. It was a problem they would both struggle with throughout their long food-based TV careers – not that it would ever stop them from enjoying chowing down on the feasts so often put in front of them during their 20-years on TV.

Mel told *The Mirror* in the year 2000: 'At the end of the first series – 12 weeks – I'd put on at least a stone-and-a-half, and my weight was up to 10 3/4 stone. It didn't show as much on Sue, because she was smaller to start off with. And she's got a massively quick metabolism. She can eat pretty much the crappest things on the planet, and it just zaps away in nervous energy.'

Mel began getting letters from fans saying how pleased they were to see that she was such a 'normal size' compared to everyone else on telly. And she even received a letter from a women's magazine asking her to take part in an article on enormous breasts.

'Everyone in the office was laughing, and I was, too,' she later said. 'I didn't tell anyone, but I went home and I was bloody pissed off, actually. I looked in the mirror and immediately saw these enormous melons. Very depressing.'

But while people were laughing, the weight-gain led to pressure being put on the pair to shed pounds and even change their image with makeovers. For Sue particularly, the experience was tough. 'There's not one ounce of me that cares about the way I look,' she told *The Scotsman* in 1998. But the big bosses were concerned by her pale skin and dark hair, which was described to her as looking 'nigh on satanic' on television according to Sue in the same interview – obviously an upsetting thing to hear.

'I thought, "I can't change that,"' she said in the interview. 'In the end, I just said, "If you've got a problem with my face, just say it. I've got dark hair – someone in television has to." You have an instinct for what's right and you've just got to learn to trust it.

She added: 'I can remember a two-hour meeting about what should be done with my unibrow. But times have moved on and for every stunning Tess Daley on the screen, there's now room for a speccy weirdo like me.

'I'm also more confident, so these days if someone brought up my appearance I'd be likely to say, "Isn't there something a bit more interesting we could be talking about?"'

For Mel, there were no comparisons with the dark arts – instead she was bothered by inferences that were being made about her weight and general comments on the shoddiness of her clothes. 'I was advised to go out and get a working wardrobe,' was how she tactfully described the issue to one journalist.

Aside from those initial battles of wills, preparing for and filming the daily show could get exhausting too, and on one occasion almost got Sue thrown off the show.

'I was tired and dropped the F-Bomb,' she revealed years later. 'I was saying goodbye, so there was lots of applause, but you could still lip read me saying, "Bye, have a fucking great weekend!" All you see is Mel turning to me with her mouth open, then both of us crying with laughter.'

It was the applause that saved her – had there been none it would indeed have been a sackable offence.

After 60 episodes the first season came to an end in May 2007. By that time, 18.4 million people had tuned in at some point to watch their antics and the show was a runaway success. Even the reviews were resoundingly positive.

The Independent described them as 'the freshest thing on television,' saying that Mel and Sue 'tread the fine line between celebrity celebration and send-up with deftness – and a daft sense of humour'.

TV critic Jaci Stephens described them as 'highly polished performers, total naturals in front of the camera and never less than a joy to watch,' in the *Daily Mail* in 1997, and predicted a bright future for them, albeit on a different channel: 'I suspect they will be snapped up by the BBC before the year is out. They would be ideal for a revamped *Noel's House Party*-style show on BBC1. They are off-the-wall, but not so off-the-wall that they would not fit in perfectly to mainstream, peak-time shows, and if BBC1 controller Peter Salmon is serious about bringing more women to BBC entertainment and comedy, Mel and Sue would be a good place to start. Sorry, Channel 4, but you know the format – you breed 'em, others nick 'em.'

But the BBC didn't steal the duo, and they were quickly signed up by C4 for a second season of *Light Lunch*, set to begin later that year. In between, they got together with Emma Kennedy and another pal, Geraldine McNulty, to do an Edinburgh Fringe show called *The Big Squeeze*.

Rehearsals took place in Bracknell, and Kennedy was in charge of getting non-drivers Mel and Sue from their homes in London to the studio in Berkshire. 'It was, without a doubt, the single most stressful job of my life,' Kennedy later recalled. 'Not because of anything to do with the show itself, but because Mel and Sue, as much as I love and adore them, were absolutely rubbish at timekeeping.'

When they were finally ready to perform it, the show was described as 'an affable if slightly old-fashioned student revue for those who want to see Mel and Sue, presenters of Channel 4's *Light Lunch*, in the flesh...'

The Independent's Nicholas Barber commented: 'The high-class thesping of Geraldine McNulty and Emma Kennedy gives *The Big Squeeze* an extra element, but it's an element which neutralises some of the central duo's chummy chemistry.'

But despite these few niggling criticisms, the four pals had the audience in the palm of their hands as they raced through an incredible 28 different characters in their allotted performance hour: it was their most successful Fringe show yet.

Back in London that autumn, Mel and Sue began filming the second series of *Light Lunch*, which proved to be even more popular than the first. They were still thoroughly enjoying the freedom of having their own show, and despite their success, still didn't take themselves too seriously. It came across in their relaxed approach to presenting and made their fans love them even more.

They played cauliflower football with Alison Steadman, simulated radio kissing with the cast of *The Archers*, and negotiated the hostile waters between Sooty and Orville. 'They were annoyed at being on the show together because they don't get on. Orville had the advantage of being able to speak,' Sue later recalled. 'Poor Sooty just had to silently "bear" it.'

Channel 4 was praised highly for their bravery in taking such a risk – two relatively unknown presenters and a show that was a perkily post-modern break from the usual sickly serious sincerity of daytime TV.

But it seems they hadn't been so brave when planning original format for the show. As Mel revealed to *The Scotsman* a year later, at the height of the show's success: 'The pilot was literally enormous bouffant hair, lots of jewellery in buffs and burgundies. We were so ill at ease sitting round a table.'

It was not to Mel and Sue's taste at all, and neither was it to the British public's. And so despite the pressure to conform to the achingly dreary daytime stereotypes, blandly discussing unoriginal topics with celebrities who either no one had ever heard of or were so overexposed they'd run out of things to say, Mel and Sue had stood their ground. And their struggle in getting the show to be accepted the way *they* envisioned it had brought the two women even closer together.

'We had so much bulls hit to wade through so we had to put on a really united front because of that,' said Mel in the same interview with *The Scotsman*. 'We admit they were taking an enormous risk by giving over five live hours a week to nobodies but there was a lot of interference. And because we were nobodies, we were a lot more malleable.'

But the women had their own agenda and were looking out

for their own interests, as well as the best interests of the show. It was important to them that they didn't weakly give in and deliver a bog-standard and boring daytime show that would be ignored and then disappear, along with their at long-last blossoming careers.

A production company can regenerate if something goes wrong with a programme you've created, you can do another project - but if you're a performer and you do something that doesn't work, you're all too often out in the cold.

After two seasons of *Light Lunch* it was obvious that they had been right all along – official viewing figures now sat more than nicely at 1.8 million, and Channel 4 had a brand new offer for the duo.

CHAPTER 7

LATE LUNCH

'We're not going to go out and get coked-up. That's not
our style. We're governed by the fear of being tossers.'
Mel Giedroyc, *The Independent*

Channel 4 was very pleased with their newest television hosts and the resounding success of their cutting-edge cookery chat show *Light Lunch*. It had quickly and firmly become part of the British consciousness, so much so that French and Saunders even parodied the duo and the programme in a sketch on their show.

It showed how proud they were of their protégées and how far they believed they had come, as well as how very real Mel and Sue's achievement with *Light Lunch* had so far been. Everybody loved it.

After careful consideration it was decided that the show deserved a much more prominent position in the schedule, and so the duo were told that it would be moved to a 6pm slot instead of the 12:30pm one they had filled so well for two seasons.

There were more changes: it would be edited down from one hour to 30 minutes and it would be screened three times a week on Tuesday, Wednesday and Thursday instead of every weekday as they were used to – although it was to be repeated the following day at lunchtime, so as not to lose the audience they had already built up.

The plan was to turn it into a sort of *TFI Wednesday* and make it the jewel of the early evening schedule. Only time would tell if the gamble of changing something so brilliant and innovative after only two seasons would do it irreparable damage or keep it fresh and make it last.

For the comedy couple, life was good. They both had enough money to support the kind of lifestyle they had only ever dreamed of, and they were actually, properly, famous. Newspapers and magazines were constantly calling for quotes and interviews, and lots of other TV work was coming in. The pair co-hosted the World AIDS Day telethon 'Live from the Lighthouse' in 1998 with Stephen Fry – a huge sign of their popularity.

Sue began to do the rounds on the celebrity panel show circuit but struggled in the male-dominated and intense environment. She had a terrifying experience on *Have I Got News for You*, where she was outspoken by all the other guests and looked strangely lost without Mel. She barely spoke all night.

'I didn't think I could be so frightened,' she told blogger Mary Comerford. 'I was paired with Ian Hislop and it was really competitive with all this wit flying around. I wasn't well-known, so the pressure to be good was more intense, but I didn't say anything for the last half-hour of the recording. At one point Ian passed me a note with "just talk" written on it.'

Mel was nothing but loyally supportive of this brief solo outing and told Sue she was brilliant', and that 'it was a long day'.

For the new *Late Lunch* format, additions were made to the original *Light Lunch* team. One of the newbies employed as an audience researcher was a then unknown Dermot O'Leary, who instantly hit it off with coquettish Mel. The duo ended up snogging at one point but nothing more happened between them.

For help with the writing side of things, the duo drafted-in their old pal Emma Kennedy to work as a script editor. With the new shorter screen-time, things would have to be a lot tighter and they knew that Emma was good at honing and shaping their work.

'It wasn't like work; it was a joy,' Emma recalled to *The Independent* in 2008, in an article about her friendship with Mel. 'We only had one work argument, when Julie Walters came on. We revere her like a goddess, and Mel and I had a tussle over who'd take her a cup of tea – Mel just looked me in the eyes and said, "I'm taking it".'

By now, Emma had been Sue's girlfriend for a while, although publicly she was never mentioned. In fact, it was only discovered that they had ever been together when Emma gave an interview to the Sapphic magazine *DIVA* in 2013. 'I went out with Sue for five years – but no one noticed,' she told them in the shock revelation.

In interviews, Sue was purposefully vague about her love life, but when probed she mentioned boyfriends past or vague dates – never revealing her true sexuality or the name of her partner.

On *Light Lunch* she had flirted with the male guests and made occasional references to boyfriends. On the very first episode of *Late Lunch*, which was aired between *ER* and *Friends*, she even said: 'And ladies and gay gentlemen, I can thoroughly recommend being sandwiched between Dr Carter and Joey Tribbiani…'

During one interview, she was asked about her love life and she said she'd been dating someone for a few months but wouldn't reveal his identity because he wasn't in the business. It was an awkward moment, which Mel diffused by joking: 'Come on Sue, it's Michael Portillo!'

To the outside world – and even to her family – she was straight. And as much as the small coterie of close friends who knew the truth tried to convince her to just be publicly honest, it would take some time before she felt she could. The process of disclosure would be fraught. It was a private matter. She didn't want to share it.

But as rumours began to rumble she knew she had to at least tell her parents – something she was absolutely terrified about.

Dad Bert and mum Ann had been so supportive of Sue's career, even when things weren't working out so well. She was now 28 and successful – she wanted desperately not to disappoint them, which she felt she would if her secret were discovered.

Eventually the fear of them reading the truth in a newspaper outweighed her fear of revealing it to them herself. That, coupled with the pressure she was receiving from her friends, pushed her to finally come clean.

'I was living with a girl who was completely straight but even she was starting to get flak. So I phoned Mum,' Sue explained to journalist Frances Hardy of the *Daily Mail* in 2005. 'There was a strangulated U-bend in my throat," she added. "You feel you're telling your family something they least expect to hear; that you're letting them down. I said, "I thought I'd come and see you tomorrow". She said, "Are you ill?" I stammered, "No, I just need to talk to you about er– something".'

Even though she had made the decision, actually getting the

words out proved a lot tougher. But devoted mother Ann knew how to coax things out of her eldest daughter.

'So she fired off a list of questions,' Sue said in the same interview. '"Have you got money problems? Are you pregnant?" Then she said, "Do you want to talk to me about your sexuality?" She stole my moment. I wanted to orchestrate my own drama.'

Sue's thunder had been well and truly stolen but it must have been somewhat of a relief.

'There was a pause. It was weird. For the first time in my life I was sexualised in front of my mum, she continued telling *the Daily Mail.* But she is a wise bird, a good, open-minded person. I think she was upset because she thought I'd make a good mum. She worried that life would not be easy for me, that I'd be damaged and hurt. But she knew if I could withstand it, she could. I've always been a bit exasperating. In the end, it was just another in the long line of things I could do to be awkward!'

Ann took responsibility for telling Sue's dad. 'His response was brilliant," Sue said in the same interview. 'He said, "Whatever makes you happy is fine by me". So my parents were wonderful and, of course, afterwards, I realised that all my panic and worry had been ridiculous.'

Although the 'big reveal' had gone well, and Sue felt like a weight had been lifted from her shoulders, she still wasn't ready to come out of the closet publicly. Instead she ignored the rising swirl of rumours and went about her new exciting media life.

After 149 successful episodes of *Light Lunch*, spin-off *Late Lunch* began on 31 March, 1998. Anyone who was anyone wanted to guest on the show: the duo interviewed Jo Brand, Jackie

Collins, Linford Christie, Whoopi Goldberg. Even Madonna was scheduled-in for an appearance, although it didn't work out.

The duo turned the situation around to their advantage: the singer had just released her latest single 'Frozen', and the duo joked that it was a case of bad timing, saying that Madonna must have been feeling intimidated, because, quite by coincidence, they had released their debut single 'It's Freezing,' that week too. Maybe she was concerned about the competition?

They then parodied the blue-filtered video of Madonna writhing around in a black veil, to much laughter from the audience. Luckily for them, the health-conscious actress Gwyneth Paltrow was only too happy to appear which apparently made for a fun show. Paltrow made a healthy drink and some cucumber sandwiches for Mel and Sue. She even cut the crusts off.

On another episode, Mel fixed morning TV heart-throb Richard Madeley with her best pseudo-serious face and declared: 'We know you're a TV god, a wonderful husband and a loving father, but what we really want to know is (there was a pause for a drum roll) Riccardo, can you play crazy golf?'

She and Sue had actually Morris-danced with excitement at the thought of watching Madeley swing his club on the show. But while they gently mocked the stars on their shows, it was their self-deprecation that lay at the heart of their appeal. They were always taking the mickey out of themselves just as much as their guests and it was when the guests started mocking them back that the duo got the biggest laughs from the audience.

They played heavily on what they perceived as their mediocrity and the fact that they didn't lead a showbiz life in the slightest. \Viewers could see how real they were and warmed to Mel and Sue instantly. In so many ways they were exactly the same on-screen with each other as they were off-screen: giggling at in-jokes, finishing each other's sentences and constantly going off on the kind of tangents that both helped and hindered their writing progress. One interviewer at the time sat with them as they seamlessly moved from Una Stubbs' woolcraft to how difficult it was to make a Jane Asher *Thomas the Tank Engine* cake in a stream of consciousness that almost left her light-headed.

Things were going so well that the only visible danger was that they would get sucked into the trap of becoming the type of celebrities that they so delighted in gently mocking, and so lose their satirical edge.

But they were smarter than that. If they had been young and green and fresh out of school when they were plucked from obscurity they might have gone down the celebrity route, but Mel was nearly 30, and Sue wasn't far behind. They already had a good group of friends and their heads were screwed on right. 'We're more grounded,' Mel said in a lengthy interview with *The Independent* at the time. 'We're not going to go out and get coked-up. That's not our style. We're governed by the fear of being tossers.'

With impeccable double-act timing, reported the newspaper, Sue chose that moment to interject with: 'The good thing is that we were tossers way before we were in the media.'

Besides, their family wouldn't have let them get away with any diva-like behaviour. 'Not a day goes by without my family ripping the piss out of me,' Mel said in the same interview. 'On Sunday my niece said to me, "My friend at school said you're a silly actress and I agree".'

Having those Jiminy Cricket-style voices abusing them definitely kept their feet on solid ground. Besides, Mel hadn't stopped wearing her trademark Beryl the Peril-style pigtails yet, while Sue couldn't get her nipples to behave, no matter how hard she and Debbie from wardrobe tried.

'I can't wear anything thin because I get terrible nipple erections on the show,' Sue admitted to *The Scotsman*. 'Not through sexual excitement,' she clarified, 'through nerves, and they just pop up.'

After Sellotaping them down, putting plasters over them and hairdryering them, Sue and Debbie gave up and just resorted to laughing. 'They pop up at the mere hint of live television and they just won't go down.'

It was the reason why Sue mainly wore big jumpers on the show, which made her breasts look huge. 'There was a particular blue chenille one that made me look like I had enormous rockets.'

Jumpers and nipples weren't the only problems on the show: the new, shorter format was proving to be a mistake and by the end of the first season neither Mel, Sue, Channel 4 or their regular viewers were happy with it.

In 30 minutes there just wasn't the space for Mel and Sue to be themselves and let their natural humour unfold. It all felt a little bit squashed and didn't have the natural pace that *Light Lunch* had.

No one wanted to see it go completely, least of all its presenters. After some in-depth discussions, and relentless campaigning from Mel and Sue, a second series of *Late Lunch* was commissioned: it would air once a week, with a running time of one hour. And this time they'd have their name in the title too.

But the format was changing again, so soon after it had already been changed once before. There were whispers in TV-land that it couldn't sustain being tinkered with any more. They'd had a winning formula in the first place – why were they messing with it?

Mel celebrated her thirtieth birthday that June with mixed feelings. She had been dreading saying goodbye to her twenties. Yes, she now was one-half of a successful comedy double act, but she was still single and worried that time was ticking by. She still desperately wanted a family and the urge to be a mother was growing painfully strong.

Her thirtieth was a big turning point but there was nothing she could do to stop it happening. So she decided to just face it head-on. 'I organised a party, marked it, and just had the best time,' she said later. 'You wake up and feel a sense of relief. Calm. And I just felt more at ease with myself.' She also went on a long holiday to sunny Greece and flirted like a teenager while she was out there.

Though the pair were growing up, they were still their silly old childish selves deep down: while Mel was trying to sort out a mortgage that autumn, Sue pulled down her jeans and pants and mooned right in her face.

As the countdown to Series 2 began in early 1999, the duo gave publicity interviews to remind their fans to tune in to the new hour-long format. They sounded excited about it.

'There'll be a lot more room to ramble,' Mel told journalists. 'A lot more arsing about, not self-indulgent but actually geeing it up.'

'A lot more goolie jokes,' was Sue's offering. 'Laughing at each other's ineptitude and our own.'

But they were remarkably vague about what the future would bring – both in the form of the guests they were expecting – 'it's a surprise,' said Mel when asked, after an awkward silence – and on what was going to happen after that series was finished.

'We'll see how it goes, really,' Sue said. 'They don't tell us until quite late on. It's entirely up to them. They might keep the franchise going without us, we don't know. It's not our idea.'

For some fans it felt like the excitement was forced and the other obscure things they were saying were almost a hint that change was on the way – yet again. In hindsight, also, this is how their interviews now come across.

But it's difficult to highlight exactly when Mel and Sue fell out of love with *Light/Late Lunch*. They certainly looked their usual effervescent selves when the trailer for the show was released.

Shot on a white background, with Mel, Sue and the band in serious black outfits, it was a beautiful parody of seriousness. Yes, they were in suits, but Sue's hair was tinged with purple and Mel's was in Baby Spice-style bunch buns. Also, they were singing and dancing. Badly. It looked like *Late Lunch* Version 2 was going to be good.

The two women forced themselves back into the all-consuming routine of writing and filming the show. On air, they were exactly the same as they had always been, and approached their interviewing roles with the same enthusiasm. They both appeared to positively drool over footballer David Ginola and actor Neil Pearson, and gently fawned over actresses Alison Steadman and Jennifer Ehle (they were both big fans). Comedians such as Bill Bailey, Norman Pace and Jeff Green bantered with the double act, while even Hollywood's very own Matthew Modine found his way onto the set.

They had their own fashion show, guest-starring Ben De Lisi, Antony Price and Lowri Turner, and joined the magic circle accompanied by the legendary Paul Daniels and his wife, Debbie McGee.

It was a rich season line-up, which ended with the eighteenth episode in March. Fans eagerly awaited the next series, but little did they know that it was the last Britain would see of the short-lived but much-loved show.

CHAPTER 8

BRANCHING OUT

*'I hope that we've shown that if two dumpsters from Surrey
can come along and be on telly for a bit, then anyone can.'*
Sue Perkins

It's difficult to get to the bottom of why a show as popular as *Light/Late Lunch* ended so abruptly. Some newspapers reported a rapid decline in viewing figures, others claimed that the comedy duo had quit and there was no one to replace them.

Mel says that it was their decision: 'We'd done it for two years and it took over our lives. We didn't see our friends or family. We were getting to the stage where we were thinking, where's our comedy going to come from?'

It would seem that this explanation is the most probable: both Mel and Sue definitely missed the excitement of stand-up and touring. 'I'm a sucker for that smelly greasepaint, roaring crowd thing,' Sue had often told interviewers.

Television could be monotonous and formulaic, while stand-up meant they could do what they wanted. They missed their freedom and wanted a change. Now that they were household names, they believed they could return to the stage and make their tours successful enough to sustain their new lifestyles.

As soon as *Late Lunch* Series 2 was over, and before it was even common knowledge that it wasn't coming back, the duo announced they were working on a new touring show to be called *Back to Our Roots*. The clue was in the name: it was stand-up, silliness and sketches, all the things they'd loved and worked so hard on in their pre-*Lunch* days.

The tour began in April in Brighton, barely a month after *Late Lunch*'s last episode was aired, and went all over the country. It was very popular and sold out most of its venues – and not only because the show offered its guests a free make-over or hairdo if they arrived early. The *Back to Our Roots* show offered a double treat: the duo's unique mix of satirical girly humour, cocky self-derision and nineties banter, and for women in the audience, the chance of getting themselves a pair of Mel pigtail buns.

The show was mainly sketch show-based, which was where Mel and Sue's true comedy passion lay. Sue was a literature scholar and a writer and Mel a serious actress at heart, and these qualities, mixed with their flair for comedy, combined best in the form of funny sketches. For this show, many of them were health- and beauty-based, hence the impromptu make-overs, which were typical of their quirky approach to comedy.

After a gap of several years, the girls were back on tour and very pleased everyone was about it too. They still displayed all the qualities that had won sofa-loads of student fans their TV chat show – most of these characteristics tending to begin with the letter 's': sassy, saucy, sussed, sarky – and they were the very embodiment of the nineties, which was fast drawing to a close.

As on TV, the pair were at their best when their professionalism was at its worst. During the sketches themselves they often lost it completely and had to step out of character to take the Mick out of each other's frequent fluffs.

'Helpless corpsing is not unknown,' read one local newspaper review. 'Rather than appearing self-indulgent – a distinct danger – this capacity to revel in their own incompetence is rather endearing.'

During one performance at The Corn Exchange in Ipswich, Mel totally forgot her lines. The duo were doing a sketch about two debutantes flat-sharing in the sixties when she just went blank, leaving Sue, once again, to pick up the pieces.

'I'm off to start a double act with Sue Pollard,' she harrumphed, diffusing the awkwardness and garnering more than a handful of guffaws.

The joke continued into the next sketch, when Mel recalled that, as the youngest member of her family, she got a lot of hand-me-downs. 'What did they hand you down?' asked Sue, arching an eyebrow. 'Not a memory, I gather.'

And mostly it was their harmless bickering, the genuine-ness of their friendship that came shining through so often, that made them just so likeable. They were like an old married couple, griping and snickering, but clearly still devoted to each other and exuding warmth and friendship.

'Like all the most memorable double acts,' wrote James Rampton in his review for *The Independent*, 'Morecambe and Wise, Reeves and Mortimer – they know that audiences prefer to see the fur fly than mutual petting... With Mel and Sue no opportunity to mock is missed.' Rampton was mostly appreciative of the duo's efforts, especially their 'commendable willingness to experiment with material'.

They sang, they danced, they wittered on about rationing and brisket and Eurovision – it was the kind of song-and-sketch show that first got them started, and it clearly still worked.

As the two presenters drove off into the comedy sunset on the two-month tour, back home in TV-land they were being hotly pursued by a variety of British broadcasters, who were mindful of the fact that they were now free and available.

'Everybody was champing at the bit to get their next project,' a TV insider told the *Daily Mirror*. It was something Mel and Sue would have to consider carefully: they wanted to keep their options open, as they weren't enamoured with the prospect of being tied to one project again. They had loved their first experience of presenting on *Light Lunch*, but after years of project-hopping before they were famous, they had found it hard to stay enthusiastic doing the same thing day-after-day.

But on the other hand, although they wanted to retain their freedom, they also needed to line up their next pay packet – they didn't want to be left out in the cold, and they knew how fickle the showbiz world could be. If they didn't stay in the public eye they would disappear for good and quickly run out of money again.

So before they had even finished their tour, they signed to Granada to present a new showbiz quiz show called *Casting Couch*, due to air later in the year. The programme had actually been designed with the pair in mind and the deal wasn't exclusive, which meant that Mel and Sue could do as many other things as they liked.

Mel narrated the Miss World coverage for Channel 5, while Sue worked on *The 99p Challenge*, a Radio 4 show which she had been presenting for a year already, and which would continue until 2004.

And it wasn't long before they struck an incredibly lucrative deal to make their first foray into the world of advertising. Allied Bakeries approached the pair to front an ad for Kingsmill Tasty Wholemeal, a new brown loaf being added to its range of breads.

The brand had identified the pair as perfect for their demographic. Marketing director Frances Brindle said at the time that, 'Kingsmill Tasty Wholemeal is targeted at younger consumers. Mel and Sue's comedy reflects the values of today's younger women and research shows younger housewives have a strong affinity with them.'

The same appeal that had made them popular on *Light Lunch* would be perfect to appeal to the same demographic that was felt would buy Kingsmill products. For Allied Bakeries it was a no-brainer, and they signed up the pair as part of a £3 million package of marketing support for the new bread. The girls got a nice slice of that loaf for their troubles too.

Filming did have its problems though, as Mel told *The Mirror*: 'They just wanted take after take,' she said. 'In the end we had to get through, or take a bite out of, ninety salmon sandwiches! I didn't have any lunch that day, which for me is saying something. And I couldn't look at a salmon for a while, either.' It was, her fans were sure she'd agree, a small sacrifice.

In the last year of the century, things were really coming together for Mel and Sue. They would be on British screens again in the autumn, which gave them the whole summer to write and rehearse, and the money from Kingsmill meant they could relax a little too and enjoy themselves.

On the last night of the *Back to Our Roots* tour in May, Mel gave up smoking for good. She had started when she was 15, given up for four years before taking it up again in her early twenties, but after spending two months in a small van with a load of friends who smoked, Mel finally saw the error of her ways.

'Cooped up, doing a lot of hours on the road, I just felt so ill. So it was quite easy,' she explained the following year.

The summer days rolled happily by – the two women met at each other's houses daily, usually at around midday, where they would ramble on for hours and probably did 'about half an hour's work', according to Mel. They were still close and in harmony with each other.

'I have a different way of going about things,' Mel once explained to *The Independent*. 'Perks will say exactly what's on her mind, everything is out there. I'm a little more seven-veils-ish. I don't give a lot away. Maybe I'm more reserved, until I have half a shandy inside me.'

And slowly, through interviews, their personalities were revealed to be much more complex than their fans would have imagined: further proof that the personas they had cultivated for *Light Lunch* – ditzy Mel, sharp Sue – had been convincing.

'I sometimes had to wait for her,' Mel said in her 1999 interview with *The Independent*, revealing a very different side to her character. 'I'm actually very anal, I always know where everything is. With Perks, trying to leave a room takes half an hour.'

They still spent their weekends together and with their mutual clique of friends. It was a laidback life style. 'Sue's a very good cook, so she'll cook or we'll go and see a film,' said Mel. 'I would like to think I still go out clubbing but I'm thirty now so my clubbing days might be behind me.'

So far, throughout the whole of their friendship and career together, they'd had only one argument – when Sue was late for a meal with Mel's parents. 'When I'm pissed off I get over-jolly,' Mel told *The Independent*. 'I said "lovely to see you", turned around a pulled a face. She caught the end of it and we rowed. I couldn't hack it if we normally argued.

'It's the nature of what we do: we need to be able to rely on each other. It comes across if there's a nasty edge between us.'

In August, they took *Back to Our Roots* to the Edinburgh Fringe, where it was extremely well received by critics – apart from one reviewer who couldn't even get their names right: 'Mel, the dark, intense one, is a whizz at tongue-twisting accents while Sue, the blonde, fluffy one, specialises in bewildered and mischievous expressions,' read the review, instantly confusing the duo. 'Occasionally Sue has a tendency to put in one tongue-twister too many. You also get the feeling some of their material has not evolved all that much since their days of student revue.'

It's safe to say they wouldn't have cried too many tears over that particular review.

In September that year, Sue marked her thirtieth birthday and she can't have been displeased with how her life was going: she owned her own London home, had a successful career – and a new girlfriend. She had split with Emma Kennedy amicably and the pair had remained friends. Meanwhile, she began dating Scottish livewire comic Rhona Cameron – and was still managing to keep her sexuality away from the prying eyes of the media.

In November, both *Casting Couch* and the Kingsmill advert aired on TV. The advert was funny and an instant hit. It played on their strengths and their weaknesses, showing them purposefully messing up their lines so that they could continue to eat more and more of the bread they were filming an advert for.

And while viewers laughed at the gag, they apparently also went out and bought the bread: Kingsmill reported that the product and brand was worth a whopping £30million just a year later.

Marketing Director Frances Brindle, pleased that the strategy was working, said: 'The wholemeal market was in decline until we launched our brand. We've attracted younger consumers in a market traditionally targeted at an older audience.'

But while they were advertising gold, *Casting Couch* wasn't quite so successful for the pair – even though that wasn't Mel and Sue's fault. It had been billed as a *They Think it's All Over*-style quiz that pitted teams of celebrity guests against each other over their Hollywood and showbiz knowledge, except that, as the *Daily Mail* wryly commented: '*Have I Got News for You* and That Smutty Sporty One Which Isn't Funny get all the "A" list guests and the rest turn up on shows like this, where they only think they're funny.'

Team captains were Radio 1 DJ Chris Moyles and socialite Tamara Beckwith, who at the time was spending most of her time in LA, and admitted she was pretty much only doing it for the money. 'Listen,' she told the *Mail on Sunday*, 'I'm being paid huge amounts of money just to sit there, so as far as I'm concerned they can have me for as many hours as they need.'

And they did need many hours, especially for the first episode, which reportedly took almost three mind-numbing hours to film – a tedious ordeal of autocue fluffs and dodgy props.

Beckwith was easy to make fun of, but as a team captain she tried not to 'over-extend herself'. 'It's not exactly rocket science, it's just fun," she said in the same interview. "There's nothing worse than someone trying to be really funny when it doesn't come naturally. When we have the run-through, if there's something I can say that's easy and snappy and I can get it out in the correct manner, then I'll try it, but otherwise not, or else it will look as if I'd just been given a line and I was saying it, and everyone will think: "Oh, I bet she never thought that up herself".'

But despite Beckwith's relaxed approach to her role, the subject matter of the show had great potential. Of all the subjects that had panel shows based on them – current affairs, sports, etc – the world of celebrity gossip was a good one to choose. Unfortunately, though, the show opened with a sweeping shot of the crane camera banging into the chandelier, which was funny the first time but had well and truly lost its charm by the end of the series.

The two teams had regular guests in the form of Marcus Brigstocke and Kevin Day, along with two other guests, who didn't feature much at all throughout the proceedings. The rounds were sufficiently varied and encompassed all the extravagance, shallowness and gossip of the celebrity world, and even had a charades round where Mel and Sue acted out a recent showbiz scoop using the medium of mime.

But despite its possibilities, for the critics, from the very first episode it was a total disappointment. The *Daily Mail*, for instance, pulled no punches in its review, writing: 'It tried to have a crack at the world of show business and failed. Hosts Mel Giedroyc and Sue Perkins are two of the funniest and most spontaneous comedians on television, but if they had been straight-jacketed and gagged they could not have looked more awkward than they did on this new celebrity panel quiz show.'

Those who had found the show funny put the newspaper's

grumpiness down to TV's sudden and absolute saturation with panel shows – every channel now had a variety of them and they had become 'samey' and monotonous. Maybe there was no way that Mel and Sue's new show could break through the quagmire of them all.

But the fact that the show was allocated a rather curious 10:30pm slot meant that not many people actually saw it, which may have been the real reason for its failure.

After all, Mel and Sue's excellent ad-libbing was nothing short of hilarious on the show, and they frequently went off on tangents similar to on *Light* and *Late Lunch*. One TV nostalgia website described the show as, 'One of ITV's better 1999 offerings', before adding, 'not that that says much.'

Casting Couch disappeared by Christmas, after just six episodes – just in time for Mel and Sue to celebrate the new millennium. A new century was dawning and it held limitless possibilities for the pair.

CHAPTER 9

LESSONS IN LOVE

'Everyone has always said: "You'll know." And I did.
It was amazing. Like a bolt from his shoes!'
Mel Giedroyc, *The Mirror.* 2000

The year 2000 was an eclectic one for the two hard-working celebrities. Sue was kept busy solo-presenting for the first time, after having been signed up to front Sky MovieMax's new 30-minute show, *Movie Babylon*, in October the year before.

Recorded in front of a studio audience, the show took a sideways look at movies and featured fellow stand-up Dave Gorman as Sue's roving reporter.

It was a peak-time show, which aired at 9:30pm on Friday nights and was followed by a Sky MovieMax film. Though it was commissioned for an initial 30-episode run it was dropped in the spring, with a spokesman saying: 'The show has simply run its natural course.'

But since Sue wasn't struggling for money, she wasn't worried: after the success of the first Kingsmill advert, she and Mel were signed up for a second, with a similarly fat fee as payment. This time they were advertising the company's Tasty Crust brand and the advert offered a humorous slice of family life.

In a parody of traditional family-oriented advertising, Sue posed as a busy housewife and mother while wearing a realistic-looking long-haired wig. Accompanied by two children, she was filmed loading bags of shopping into a car, saying that her friends always ask her how she finds the time to bake her own delicious bread.

The next scene saw her pretending to take a loaf from the oven, before proudly explaining that her bread-baking prowess made her popular with her family. Mel then exposed Sue as a fake, snatching the wig from her head and revealing that the 'home-baked' bread is in fact Kingsmill's Tasty Crust loaf. The ad ends with the line, 'Fresh thinking from Kingsmill'.

Marketing Director Frances Brindle was happy with the new advert, saying: 'We're looking to build a brand identity that's different from traditional bread advertising. We want to be more modern and to impress real families. We don't want to be seen as taking ourselves too seriously. Mel and Sue appeal to our target audience – families with children. They're humorous and down-to-earth.'

But while the ad targeted families and was popular with mums, it was poignant that, as yet, neither of the ad's stars was a mum herself. For Mel in particular the situation was growing more exasperating and emotionally painful. But it wouldn't be for long.

That summer, soon after turning 31, Mel found herself dating someone. And this time it felt like it was really going somewhere. Interviewed by *The Mirror* in July, it was obvious that Mel was well and truly in love. Being so head over heels had seemingly made her reflective of the previous decade of her private life, which she didn't recall too fondly, overall. But because of her now sunnier outlook in general, she was starting to see those years as stepping stones to where she now was, which was a very good place indeed.

'My relationships were always quite crap,' she told the *Daily Mirror*, 'until recently. I've met someone who has just made my life so brilliant. Gotta say, took a while. In my twenties I was all over the shop, always slightly running away. You really do start to believe that you're not meant to be with anyone.'

'I do get prone to downers,' she mused. 'And there were real ones in my twenties. Never too scary, but now I wish I'd gone and talked to somebody about it. But I'm quite sort of stiff-upper-lip, and "Come on, just go and do some gardening, or something". I've had moments of real smelly bad old luck. But it's always turned out for the best, and I've always thought, a year later, "Oh, I'm glad that didn't work out".'

Mel didn't name her new man – she didn't want to jinx what was turning into a true whirlwind romance. But eventually his name was revealed as Ben Morris, a few months older than Mel, a writer and director who was studying at film school. He was also the younger brother of the successful British satirist Chris Morris, creator of the black-humoured *The Day Today* and the brilliantly innovative and awkward *Brass Eye*, now both considered 1990s classics.

They'd met at a dinner party thrown by Chris's other half, the actress turned literary agent Jo Unwin, specifically to bring the two of them together. Nothing happened that night, but for Mel it was love at first sight – of his shoes, that is. 'They were very battered,' she recalled, wistfully. 'Like little boats, old really floppy kind of moccasin things. Very familiar somehow. I remember looking down – very strange – and saying: "I like your feet".'

They bumped into each other completely by chance shortly afterwards and Mel knew there was something unique between them. 'It was very bizarre," she said in the same interview with *The Mirror*. There was a very strong sensation of "This is something very exciting". I've never really experienced that before. Everyone has always said: "You'll know". And I did. It was amazing. Like a bolt from his shoes!'

She referred to Ben as 'Mr Shoes' to save his blushes at that early stage of their relationship. But the fact that it was the first time she'd mentioned any boyfriend with any amount of specificity told those closest to Mel a lot about how she truly felt.

'He's incredibly kind and very funny and down-to-earth,' she gushed. 'He's just great.'

Though the couple were still living apart – they'd only just met, after all – Mel was remarkably confident about the direction they were going in. 'The shoes are still round at his,' she continued in the *Mirror* interview. 'But I think there will be some mixed shoe action in the future. It's looking pretty good. The forecast is sunny with a few showers. Oh God, I can't believe I've just made a weather forecast analogy. That's so cheesy. Terrible. But that's what lurve does for you, I guess.'

All in all, Mel was definitely in a good place. She'd clocked up about 200 hours of live TV in just a few years and that figure would only rise. And coincidentally, the reason for the revealing interview in *The Mirror* happening in the first place was because Mel was fulfilling another one of her dreams. She was starring in a sitcom called *Rhona*, about a Rhona – Rhona Cameron, Sue Perkins' girlfriend.

As she told the newspaper: 'If you'd said to me when I was 21, "You'll be acting in a sitcom in ten years", I'd never in a thousand million years have believed you. I wouldn't call it acting on my part, though. It's a vague attempt to stand in the right place, look in the right camera and frankly, remember the lines. But I've got real high hopes for it.'

Many people shared her high hopes for the show. It was being touted as groundbreaking British television – the country's first sitcom featuring a lesbian star, and as such was getting a lot of publicity.

Rhona Cameron was both the heroine and the joint creator of the show, which was being compared to the US show *Ellen* before it was even aired. She also both co-wrote it – along with ex-girlfriend Linda Gibson – and sang its theme tune.

Loosely based on her own life, it centred around 'Rhona Campbell', a single, self-obsessed Scottish lesbian living in London, and her two heterosexual best friends, Lisa and Geoff. Mel played Lisa, while Geoff was portrayed by Dave Lamb.

Cameron's sexuality was not the absolute focus of the show – it was never meant to strike any kind of blow for sexual politics, but most people thought that the comic wouldn't have minded if it had. The feisty, funny comedian knew that doing the sitcom would bring with it a fair amount of stick from the press, but she was ready for it. 'I'm expecting a complete slagging off by some people, certainly by the very right-wing press. That's bound to happen,' she told the *Birmingham Post*.

'I seem to be one of the few women on the planet, in the media, who doesn't mind saying the words "I am a lesbian". I'm gay but it doesn't mean I come with all the baggage that people expect lesbians to come with.'

Cameron had never been afraid to be a lesbian and proudly claimed it as simply a part of who she was, not a secret to be kept or something special to be endlessly discussed.

'I've never intended to wave a banner or make a bit political statement,' she said in the same interview. "I'm the first lesbian I ever knew in the world. I was just like that from when I was very young and sleeping with girls was a normal part of growing up for me.'

Rhona told the *Post* interviewer, Graham Keel, that gay men weren't judged like lesbians, saying that people think of Graham Norton, for example, as an Irish chat show host. 'I don't think they ask him all the time about being gay, but I get it a lot.'

Keel wrote that it was the price Rhona was paying for her openness, and mused: 'There must be more lesbian actresses, lesbian TV presenters and lesbian newscasters but can anyone name one? If they exist, they're still right at the back of the closet.'

Which, ironically, is exactly where Cameron's own girlfriend was. And although Sue must have been proud of her success, with all the publicity flying around about Cameron's sexuality, it must have made Sue very nervous her secret was going to come out.

They argued about their different opinions on their sexuality: Cameron couldn't understand what Sue was so afraid of, while Sue just wasn't ready to share her private feelings with the world. And with journalists asking the obvious question of Rhona Cameron – who are you dating? – she knew it was bound to come out eventually.

Instead of getting ahead of the situation and going public with their relationship, Sue buried her head in the proverbial sand: she asked that Rhona not reveal her identity and, at the time, the Scottish comic agreed and stayed true to her word.

When Aiden Smith interviewed Cameron for *The Scotsman*, all she would say was that the lady in her own life was 'in the media'. But journalists are diggers, and it wasn't long before reporters at the newspaper figured out that it was Sue Perkins.

Rhona never hid her girlfriend away, despite Sue's misgivings – on the contrary, the two were spotted out together quite regularly. And when Mel and Sue appeared on *Stars in their Eyes* at around the same time, Cameron went along to support her other half. While the duo tackled Elaine Paige and Barbara Dickson – both gay icons – by singing 'I Know Him So Well', the camera panned to where the celebrities' husbands, wives, girlfriends etc were sitting, and zoomed in on Cameron in a not-so-subtle move.

When they were out, they didn't keep their public displays of affection discreet either. In July, just days before *Rhona* first aired on BBC 2, *The Scotsman* wrote in its Diary section: 'Hollywood confidential? Forget about it. For the latest in showbiz gossip look no further than the Diary. In today's exclusive we reveal who might be the latest click of the gay comic Rhona Cameron. A wee clue was on *Celebrity Stars in their Eyes* last Saturday night,' it read, before pointing out that Cameron was spotted in the audience. And even more revealingly, it then went on: 'The pair were spotted canoodling in the DJ box at the Tackno club in Embra's Market Street not so long ago.'

Sue must have been waiting in horror for the mainstream press to come knocking on her door for confirmation, but nothing really happened after the *Scotsman*'s revelation. Rather than an explosive firework, it was more of a damp squib. In fact, it went completely under the radar and Sue managed to remain firmly in the closet. Her secret also remained intact throughout *Rhona*'s six-episode run, possibly, in hindsight, because the show sadly bombed.

Rhona's script was described as 'inferior' and the acting 'wooden' and it was banished to the TV graveyard after only one series. Thus, Sue was given another temporary respite from the weight of discovery.

Cameron may not have been able to understand Sue's reservations about going public with her sexuality, but it's not difficult to see what a huge thing it would be for her after so many years of effectively pretending to be straight. The media's attitude to homosexuality was very fluid at the time, as it was moving through a period of transition. As *The Scotsman* had written a few months before, gay TV was finally 'losing its queer veneer'.

Ever since BBC2's *Gaytime TV* had been launched in 1995, television had slowly been turning a lighter shade of pink: Michael Barrymore had staggered out of the closet, Julian Clary had presented *Mr & Mrs*, Lily Savage had presented *Blankety Blank* and Dale Winton was now fronting pretty much everything.

Every sitcom and soap opera now had a gay character and storyline and the aforementioned US show *Ellen* even had a lesbian as its protagonist. In the UK, the British sitcom *Gimme Gimme Gimme* (in which Mel and Sue played characters called Beverly-Jane and Beverley-Ann in one 1999 episode) had a gay man as its main character.

'True, *Ellen* has been cancelled and *Gimme Gimme Gimme* should have been,' wrote *The Scotsman*, 'but in both cases it was humour that was lacking, not heterosexuality.'

In the late 1990s/early 2000s, any time was fast becoming gay time, which was celebratory news for the fully integrated society that had so long been hoped for.

But now that everyone knew it was 'okay to be gay', TV needed a different message about homosexuality, lest it start to sound patronising – or worse, have the opposite effect of being so outdated that it began to alienate people and push them further back into the closet.

It needed to portray homosexual people as more than just a

group of camp clubbers or butch lesbians, living outlandish and glamorous lives in bustling cities. It needed to reach the teenagers in their bedrooms in towns and quiet villages all over Britain, coming to terms with their sexuality and desperate not to feel alone with their feelings.

Channel 4's acclaimed drama *Queer As Folk* was a huge step in the right direction: its lead actors were straight and it was watched by at least as many straight people as gay. By 2000 it was into its second series and was successfully crossing the boundaries for gay men and moving them into the mainstream.

Sadly, *Rhona* – though perfectly timed for a much-needed lesbian version – didn't quite have what was necessary to move things forward for gay women, and it would be a few more years before the media moved on from simply being 'loud and proud' to having something more substantial to say about our society's wide diversity.

And because it wasn't quite all the way there yet, Sue (neither a camp clubber nor a butch lesbian) would continue exactly as she was.

And that was entirely her choice.

CHAPTER 10

BABY AND BOOM

*I was four-and-a-half months pregnant going
up the aisle. We did it all in six weeks.'*
Mel Giedroyc, *The Daily Mail*

By 2001, both Mel and Sue increasingly found themselves working on separate projects, and as they headed into their early thirties, their lives were moving in different directions too. This was no reflection on their friendship, which was still holding strong, but was a natural part of the process of getting older and wanting different things out of life.

Sue was now living with girlfriend Rhona Cameron in North London, although their relationship was strained. Mel was totally and utterly in love with her moccasin man, Ben, and they had even bought a huge house together in West London, borrowing an eye-watering £500,000 from the bank to complete on the purchase.

The repayments were steep, but Mel had money coming in and things were going well workwise. The comedy duo had filmed another lucrative Kingsmill advert together, featuring Sue being lowered, *Mission Impossible*-style into a family's living room with a bowl of healthy fruit, before Mel accidentally sends her skywards again when she blows a whistle by accident.

With the Kingsmill adverts still bankrolling them, they could afford to do whatever work they liked.

Sue appeared on an episode of *Clive Anderson Now*, guest-presented an episode of *Liquid News*, and appeared as a talking head on numerous documentaries including *I Love a 1970s Christmas*, the *I Love 1980s* series, the *I love 1990s* series, and *Annie Goes to Hollywood*. She played Dr Lloyd in one episode of *Casualty*, featured in an episode of Michael Barrymore's sitcom *Bob Martin*, and appeared on the panel of *A Question of TV*, as well as being on *Countdown* for a week and narrating a documentary celebrating 3,000 episodes of the show.

Mel also appeared as a talking head on most of the same documentaries, and guest-hosted a show called *Up Late* with Sue. She also narrated *Bad Hair Days* on her own, and during the long hot summer, filmed *Tell It 2 Me Straight*, a show which challenged volunteers over whether they really knew what their friends thought of them – be it good or bad.

Mel presented the five-part series and although you wouldn't have known it to watch the show, she found it a struggle – because unbeknownst to viewers, she was pregnant with hers and Ben's first child. It was the start of a new stage of life for Mel and the fulfilment of a longing that had consumed her for years.

'It was like, "Hooray! Now I can eat for two, or even three, let's call it four". I'd been working for ten years and I was ready to put my feet up,' she later told the *Newcastle Journal*.

But it was bad news for her working relationship with Sue: their freelance TV work had only really been intended to keep them financially afloat while they worked on finally becoming the stand-up comedy partnership they'd always envisioned. They wanted a sketch show, that was their aim, and with this in mind they'd been trying to get back to what they knew best: stand-up.

The duo had devised a new, live 24-date show, called *A Night With Mel and Sue*, to tour that autumn. It promised a new range of comic characters and had been due to kick off at the City Varieties in Leeds on 13 November 2001. But however badly they wanted it to work, and however hard they worked on new material, Mel's blossoming pregnancy would significantly hinder the process. In September, Mel publicly announced her pregnancy and the pair subsequently announced the tour's cancellation.

Touring is a strenuous experience – different beds every night, eating unhealthy food, long car journeys... Mel had wanted the child whose tiny heart was already beating inside her for nearly a decade, there was no way she was going to chance anything happening to her precious baby.

Sue understood that, although it was a definite blow. She did land another advertising contract, but this time only her vocal cords would be needed – to voice the character of Maggie the London pigeon in that year's new PG Tips advert. The brand had sidelined their famous chimps to make room for a family of birds, created by hugely successful animation company Aardman Animations, best known for *Wallace and Gromit* and *Chicken Run*.

And as there was no fanfare announcing the celebrities who voiced the characters, Sue's turn as Maggie largely went unnoticed.

She has voiced a number of characters since, including Messenger Bird in *Dinotopia*, and one of the Sparky Twins (with Mel) in the children's TV show *Little Robots*.

As 2001 turned into 2002, while Mel was four-and-a-half months pregnant, she hastily married her whirlwind love, Ben. The wedding was lovely, but not really her dream day.

'I made all the wrong choices,' she reflected later, in 2013 to the *Daily Mail*. 'Wrong haircut, wrong dress, wrong make-up, wrong everything hastily put together… we did it all in six weeks. I've said to Ben I want to do it all again. No make-up, shift dress, barefoot.'

But when you're in love those things don't matter: in just two years Mel had gone from thinking she'd be a lonely spinster all her life to being married and expecting her first child – she was blissfully happy and the details of her wedding day were insignificant. It was enough just to be together as man and wife, and about to start a family.

In May, Mel gave birth to her daughter, Florence, and her life changed forever. Sue was one of the first people to hold little Flossie, as she was nicknamed, and was proud to be asked to be her godmother. But holding the tiny baby in her arms awoke in Sue a deep yearning to be a mother herself – something that she knew would be more complicated for her to achieve than it had been for Mel.

While Mel's life was the picture of domesticity, Sue's was in turmoil. Things weren't going right with Rhona Cameron, and she wasn't working on anything with her comedy partner either, because of the new addition to Mel's family, which only added to her feelings of sadness and concern.

And while she'd managed to keep her relationship with Cameron under wraps, newspaper suspicions were still being aroused and articles mentioning their 'friendship' were becoming more frequent.

In August, an item in *The Mirror* revealed: 'Born in a home for unmarried mothers in Dundee in 1965, Rhona now shares a £400,000 home with fellow funnygirl Sue Perkins of TV's *Mel and Sue*.

'[She left Scotland] for London, where she struck up a close friendship with Perkins. Now they share a flat in trendy Belsize Park, North London.

'The pair recently attended their friend Sophie Ward's gay wedding and co-hosted a sing-a-long version of *The Sound of Music...*'

The newspapers were both hinting and fishing for information. It was obvious they were convinced about the relationship but didn't have the proof or enough of a public interest argument to publish it as fact. If Sue didn't want anyone to know about her sexuality, what right was it of anyone's to make it public just for the sake of it?

Soon after, the issue became moot – when the pair finally ended their relationship and separated. Sue, still nursing an urge to become a mother, got herself a beagle puppy, who she named Pickle. She went for long, soothing walks with the pup on London's picturesque Hampstead Heath, a stone's throw from her flat, and tried to stay under the radar while she nursed her broken heart.

When Flossie was four months old, Mel tentatively began taking steps to start work again. She and Ben needed the money: their mortgage was huge and they had even had to start taking in lodgers to pay it. She may not have wanted to tear herself from her beautiful baby, but she had to.

Mel and Sue got themselves a brand new weekly Radio 4

show, called *That Mel and Sue Thing*, where they could write and perform sketches to their heart's content. They were both relieved to be going back to what they loved best and threw themselves into their work.

The result was a series of sketches, songs and satire that soon collected a small raft of fans. Highlights included an adaptation of Jane Austen's 'lost novella, *Sweet Fanny Adams*', in which the main characters were constantly fainting; the recurring murder mystery sketch 'Leather Island'; various nations' badly sung Eurovision entries; and a series of funny public service announcements that peppered the six-part show.

But stripped of the ad-libs and mistakes that marked their live work, the show was strangely sterile. It was entirely scripted and had some great material, but with Mel and Sue hiding fully behind the characters they'd created, it wasn't quite as funny as when they were just being themselves.

Their charm lay in their live qualities, their ability to riff off each other and pick themselves up when they fluffed their lines. It would have worked better live on stage, was the view of most reviewers. Most people definitely preferred the Saturday lunchtime BBC London show they also presented at the same time, which was much more like the old days of *Light Lunch*. Together the duo would interview celebs and interesting people, chat about current affairs and ramble on without any kind of a script. It was hugely entertaining.

At the same time, they also worked on revising the show they had planned to tour with before Mel became pregnant, and eventually announced a short series of West End dates in October and November – at the Arts Theatre. They also planned to take the show to Brighton's Komedia. It was only a handful of dates, but Mel's time was still somewhat limited because of her recent motherhood.

Meanwhile, Sue had remained friends with her ex-girlfriend Rhona Cameron, and in the autumn she heard that she was going to Australia to be on a new survival-type show being made by ITV. Sue wished her luck and Cameron duly boarded the plane for the 24-hour flight, leaving Sue to get on with her life.

Little did she know that before she saw Cameron again, the well-guarded secret of her sexuality would be well and truly out.

CHAPTER 11

FACING FEARS

*'"Outing" is a very emotional phrase and I certainly didn't
feel she did that. She disclosed things about us when we'd been
together that I wished she hadn't. That's all. So I think it's
worth correcting – it's technically not true.'*
Sue Perkins, *Time Out*, 2013.

Part of the reason Rhona Cameron went on *I'm a Celebrity,
Get Me out of Here*, was as a distraction from her split from Sue.
The lengthy relationship had been intense and the two women
had been deeply and passionately in love. It would be a long time
before either of them got over the separation.

Being in the claustrophobic surroundings of a reality TV show,
with people you barely know, eating disgusting food or being
deprived of anything to eat at all, wouldn't exactly be easy. But
it was the first series of the show and no one really had a clue
what to expect. For all Cameron knew, she was raising money
for charity, in the peaceful surroundings of a beautiful jungle,
the other side of the world from her shredded personal life – it
probably sounded like the perfect way to start moving on.

In reality, Cameron found the experience very difficult indeed.
Her fellow celebs on that first, eye-opening season of the show

were Nigel Benn, Tara Palmer-Tomkinson, Christine Hamilton, Nell McAndrew, Darren Day and Uri Geller – probably the most random bunch of celebs ITV could put together.

There were tears and blazing rows right from the beginning, and by the end of the first series ratings had hit an astonishing 11 million.

Darren Day and Tara Palmer-Tomkinson rowed incessantly over his constant farting, Nigel Benn called Christine Hamilton two-faced, and Cameron described the first week as 'utterly miserable'. She was used to her own space, and being such a strong character she found it hard to tolerate some of the celebrity behaviour and attention-seeking outbursts of her jungle-mates. She wasn't about to stay quiet about it either.

Former boxer Benn nicknamed her 'Rhona the Moaner' and the pair had numerous run-ins. Cameron even accused him of bullying and homophobia. At one point, born-again Christian Benn told her she was lucky she was a woman, otherwise he'd have knocked her out. Darren Day jumped on the bandwagon and said he'd have joined in too, which was all too much like 'real' reality for Rhona's ally, Uri Geller, who expressed fears that Benn actually was going to hit the diminutive Scot.

At least there was eye-candy in the form of Tara, who half-starved Rhona clearly had a bit of a crush on. British viewers were entranced by the jaw-dropping rows, the personal revelations and the horror on the celebs' faces when they were forced to do scary or disgusting trials for their meagre food rations.

Rhona's insightful impressions of her fellow campers were a hit too and she made it to the halfway point of the show before she was kicked off. To Sue's relief, while most of the other celebs had poured their hearts out over their relationships or revealed intimate details of their personal lives, Rhona hadn't mentioned her or their former relationship once.

And instead of going out with the other evictees who were knocking on the door of her hotel room, Rhona decided to spend her first night out of the jungle alone – and on the phone to Sue. The situation that followed has been since misreported countless times as Rhona having announced that Sue was gay live on the show – this didn't happen.

But once Rhona was out of the jungle, the newspapers were clamouring for exclusives from the comic, and she didn't disappoint. It was in these interviews that Rhona referred to the heartbreak she was feeling over her recent split – not as the sole focus of the interview, but as part of where she was at that moment in her personal life.

'What viewers didn't know,' revealed the *Sunday Mail* on 8 September 2002, 'as they watched her hilarious impressions of fellow campers, was that the comedienne was hiding a secret heartache. She told no one that her three-year romance with fellow comic Sue Perkins – of TV double act Mel and Sue – had ended…'

'I wouldn't talk about my love-life because I don't need to brandish that around national television,' Cameron said in the interview. 'It had nothing to do with coming on the programme. Sometimes in life people need privacy to resolve things so I didn't want to speak about it to anyone. I'm not in a particularly settled place right now with my love life.'

Referring to Sue, she said: 'I've just come out of a very long relationship. I haven't made my peace with that yet. We're very much the love of each other's lives and although we have seen other people since, there is still some unresolved stuff. But I did speak to Sue when I got out. We've still got things to talk about.'

After the interview was published there was no way that Sue could hide from the revelation – however hard she tried. She refused to give comments when the newspapers came calling and instead wondered what on earth she was going to do.

'I'm glad I did it,' Cameron concluded about going on the show in the same interview. 'The way I look at it, if you liked me before, you probably like me a bit more. If you hated me before, you probably loathe me now. And if you had never heard of me before, you now know my name.'

Cameron duly had a surge in popularity and a boost to her career, which, she admitted, had been stalling. But it had even more dramatic effects for Sue. Though she had been photographed with Cameron before and hadn't hidden her relationship except in the press, having her sexuality finally made public was a life-changing event.

She went to ground, almost as if she felt that if she herself didn't admit it, it wouldn't be accepted as truth. She was upset at the situation. 'It was my responsibility and if I have any regrets it is that I took a long time to do it [come out],' she mused in an interview with *The Herald* a year later. 'But maybe that makes me very representative of gay people.'

The problem was, Sue had built up 'the big reveal' to be so much more than it actually was. In reality, she was just another person who was more in tune with their own sex than the opposite one. Sue had deserved to be able to keep her private life private and now she had no control over the media's scrutiny of it. Her emotions were in turmoil. She was stuck, with no idea what to do next in order to move on. Then, along with the endless newspaper interview requests, came a surprise rush of job offers from TV bosses – including the *Celebrity Big Brother* team. The new series would start shortly and after Rhona Cameron's explosive reality TV turn, they felt that Sue would be a perfect housemate.

She instantly said no. She had always been a private person and she knew that being on *Big Brother* was like being offered up as a sacrifice to the public. But she was also aware that she'd made no comment on the Cameron situation and needed something to take the focus off it and back onto her as a person and performer – maybe it would give people a chance to see the real Sue?

Cameron, who was still close to Sue, was positive about the experience. 'We talked about it and I told her that I don't think she'll have any problems in there,' she told *The Sunday Mail*. 'This is quite a big thing for Sue because she's quite shy and private. She is not an explosive person. She's a pacifier – we're very different in that score. We're similar in our souls and our humour but we're different in lots of ways.'

Eventually Sue agreed to go on the show, jokingly saying in an interview on the CH4 programme: 'I decided to do it so people might finally realise which one's Mel and which one's Sue.' Sue's fans were confused about the whole Cameron situation and hoped that while on *Big Brother* they would hear from the woman herself and finally understand what was going on in her personal life.

Sue filmed a short VT (video insert) to be shown before she went into the house, and on it were a pair who were helping her through those difficult months the most: Mel and her puppy Pickle.

Pickle was lovably naughty on camera and Sue's affection for the tiny bouncing pup was obvious. 'This is my pride and joy,' she managed, through the onslaught of licks Pickle was subjecting her to.

Mel, alternatively, was filmed raking Sue's garden as if she were the hired help – a play on the fact that Sue was going into the house as a 'famous person', when actually she was as down-to-earth as it got.

She avoided the subject of her sexuality in the video but did use humour to take a sideways swipe at the media's approach to celebrities and reality TV in general: 'Friends have asked me how I will respond to the inevitable criticism I'll get from the show, and I've merely said I'm not very bright, so most of the things that are levelled at me I simply won't understand.'

In late November, the VT was aired and Sue entered the Big Brother house. With her were presenter Anne Diamond, ex-Take That heartthrob Mark Owen, busty model Melinda Messenger, game-show host Les Dennis, and singer and artist Goldie.

The Scotsman's Tom Lappin gave Sue odds of 6-1 to win, alongside a withering summary of her career and her life so far: it was needlessly cruel and dramatic but what made it worse was that it did actually touch on elements of the self-doubt that Sue must have been feeling at the time.

> *The extent to which she has impinged on popular culture may or may not be gauged by the fact that I always thought she was Mel, and her bubbly, irritating blonde sidekick was Sue* [began Lapin, somehow mistaking ignorance for wit].
>
> *But that doesn't matter. In truth, we like Sue, and suspect she may emerge victorious from this inglorious popularity contest. What is appealing is that she carries her disappointment around on her face. She never developed the showbiz smile, that rictus leer of insincerity. Sue's default expression is pissed-off. You can read the shame she carries with her, that deep*

sense of self-disappointment that she turned a promising Fringe comedy talent into daytime TV moron-fodder.

You can see she knows she's faded now, that there is a deep sadness at attempting to carry on with the student humour when you're pushing into middle-age. You sense that she has agreed to do Big Brother *because she feels she deserves it – the logical conclusion of a career spent cheerfully accepting the bland buck. And because they weren't queuing to cast her as the next Bond girl.*

In between the outright nastiness levelled towards the talented and intelligent woman (obviously composed to get a reaction), some of what *The Scotsman*'s Lappin wrote rang a small and painful bell of truth: she was in between relationships, in an in-between phase of her career, and half in, half out of the closet. She would turn things around in just a few years' time, but if she were to be honest with herself, she would admit that these were indeed fallow years.

Sue lasted nine miserable but remarkable days in the *Big Brother* house, and when she came out she was finally free from her own demons – and free at last to live her life completely out in the open.

Most people remember that series of *Celeb Big Brother* for Les Dennis's depression and near breakdown over his split from Amanda Holden. But without a doubt the most important moment overall was when Sue publicly outed herself live on national TV.

Most people didn't really warm to Sue on the show, as (probably in no small part due to clever editing) after the first few days she came across as grumpy and sullen. But she had been thrust into a house full of perky celebs and next to megawatt Melinda Messenger – who was trying her best to be as stereotypically blonde and bubbly as possible – it would have been hard to appear anything but less chirpy.

Also, like everyone else, Sue was homesick. Who wouldn't find it hard?

On Day Six, her time under house arrest had finally proved introspective enough for Sue to begin talking as if the cameras weren't running, which is, after all, what the show is geared towards.

In a late-night chat with Mel, Les and eventual winner Mark Owen, she started to finally be open about her relationship with Cameron, and consequently her sexuality. She explained how she felt about Cameron revealing they were together to the press.

'Rhona sold her story when she came out of the jungle and effectively outed me,' she told the celeb gang. 'Which is my right to do. There was a reason I deliberately avoided it,' she explained of her decision to keep her sexuality private for so long. 'I spent years dealing with it. Basically, I think society has moved on to a point where you don't have to make these dramatic declarations. Nobody gives a toss!'

Except that a small part of Sue still clearly believed that they did and was frightened of the consequences. And she was also clearly still unhappy with how Cameron had spoken to the newspapers. 'Prior to coming in here, I know that whatever's written about me will be infused with that,' she said.

'If someone you've been with for a while does that to you, you just have to let them do it. It's your conscience. I just thought, would I do that to her? No. Will I be going around doing that to her afterwards? No.'

'But you're different,' said Mark, trying to be sympathetic. Sue said that she had spent a long time trying to understand why her ex had spoken to the press. 'I've had a safer, better life,' she concluded. 'Her principles are different – they've had to be. So I don't judge her too harshly,' she said.

She was referring to the fact that while she had been brought up in a loving middle-class home in the leafy suburbs of London, Cameron had been born in a home for unmarried mothers in Dundee. They had clearly experienced very different childhoods. She also revealed that life with Cameron towards the end had been difficult, describing the last year particularly as being like 'a war'.

And although it felt better to get it all out, as soon as she'd finished Sue panicked. Had she really just outed herself on camera? It was late at night, could she make them edit the revealing chat out? She went to the diary room and asked the producers to please not air the conversation. But it was far too good a few minutes of juicy screen-time to be chopped out, and so when it was aired not long after, Sue finally outed herself to millions of *Big Brother* viewers and consequently the whole of Britain.

After that, her final three days in the house were not pleasant. She had thought it would be interesting and a challenge to live under the spotlight with people she didn't know. Her natural inquisitiveness had even been a little excited at the prospect, imagining interesting chats and possibly even new friendships.

But she had never expected the level of boredom she'd experience without being able to exercise her mind, and on top of this she had now admitted she was gay to the whole nation – and she had no idea how they were reacting to the news.

She later said to the *Evening Standard*: 'I've never been without a pen and paper before in my life. You don't know what boredom is until you've been in the house – how people do it for 10 weeks is beyond me.' Also, she wasn't the kind of person to play the fame game – putting on an act for the public – so she found it hard to be around some of the other celebs, who she felt were doing exactly that.

The day after her public revelation, homesick, worried and desperate to leave, Sue was definitely showing signs of strain and she had an understandable little cry. Soon after, she went into the diary room and vented her spleen for nearly half an hour.

She called Melinda Messenger a 'blonde Vulcan', described Les Dennis as 'the Dark Lord of the Showtune', and said that she herself should be voted out because she had become boring.

'I was really hoping the evictions would be tonight,' she began. 'I do find it difficult with certain people because I feel I have nothing in common with them. I can't get through on any meaningful level to either Melinda or Les.

'She's the blonde Vulcan, batting her eyelids. I find her hard to talk to. Every time I talk to her about things that are important or really matter, she looks at me like I'm narrow-minded or upset. She just starts talking to me like I'm a child. She gives nothing away. I'm not saying I dislike her but I won't confide in her.'

She said she was finding it hard to cope with not having any cigarettes in the house and couldn't handle the feeling of competition. 'I don't think in here I'm capable of being myself. I would rather go, and have a reality check and a laugh. If I try and have a laugh in here, I sense a lot of resistance from Les because that's his job and I just back off. He's the Dark Lord of the Showtune.

'I don't want to compete. I can't be bothered to compete for attention or approval and Les is desperate for approval and that's why he gets upset. It's a classic performer's neurosis.

'To be honest I don't believe the public care whether I cry or not. The public will look at the pretty face and stability of Mel. They won't give a *****.'

A bleep concealed exactly which expletive Sue had decided to use to punctuate her missive.

At the end of the tirade, she was told: 'Big Brother doesn't think you've gone mad. We're caring and hoping you enjoy the remainder of your time in the house.'

It's safe to say she didn't.

On one occasion, when she took a defrosted chicken that she thought had gone off into the diary room to ask for advice, Big Brother asked her what she would do in a normal situation. Quick as a flash she replied: 'Well in a normal situation I wouldn't have Les Dennis in my house.'

On the penultimate day of the competition, Sue put on her coat in hopeful preparation and waited for Davina McCall to announce who was going home.

She looked exhausted, but put on a brave face while she waited for the news. And when it came, she looked relieved. It seemed like the public had heard her pleas: she was voted out with a huge majority of 75.8 per cent of the 257,115 votes.

Sue was too cerebral and sensitive and cared too little about winning to have ever enjoyed *Big Brother*. Instead it reminded her of everything she hated about fame and celebrity. She wanted to be respected and admired for her talents, but they had no room to shine in the stifling surroundings of the *Big Brother* house.

'I felt vulnerable,' she explained to *The Scotsman* a few years later. 'It brought out the sadder, more wistful, boring parts of my personality. I'm quite a vivacious person really, I like conversations and jokes and I couldn't get any of that going. There's a deadening of the environment in there, and it wasn't helped by my mood at the time.'

Upon leaving, she was greeted by her sister Michelle and her best mate Mel. It was an emotional reunion, drawing a line under an equally emotional few months.

CHAPTER 12

THE AFTERMATH

*'Sadly, exactly what I had expected after being on
Big Brother has happened; in one week I've gone from being one
half of Mel and Sue to being a lesbian comic.'*
Sue Perkins, *The Evening Standard*

When Sue left the house she was relieved to get back home to her puppy Pickle and the safe surroundings of her own, cosy Belsize Park flat.

She apologised to Rhona Cameron for what she'd said in the house, and got back to work right away, teaming up with Mel to work on their new stand-up show, *Mel and Sue 2002 Live*. Mel had been supportive of Sue throughout the previous few months – from break-up to *Big Brother* – despite her own fears concerning Sue going on the reality show. She had seen what going on a show like that could do for someone's career – the exposure had catapulted countless relative unknowns into the celeb stratosphere, and although she wished nothing but the best for her troubled pal Sue, she was worried it would mean the end of their partnership.

'I did find it quite tough because I thought, "Oh my God, this is the end of us as a duo because it's going to propel her into this big spotlight",' she told the *Newcastle Chronicle* two years later.

Mel was wise enough to understand that their lives would ultimately always take different directions – she herself was enjoying motherhood and while Sue had Pickle to look after, she had much more time to focus on work than Mel did. Mel didn't want to be left behind – the duo had always done things together – but she would be happy for Sue if her career did take off ahead of her own.

'I would stalk her, I would make her life a misery and slash her tyres,' she joked in the same interview. 'No, seriously, I hope that I'd be big enough to enjoy it for her.'

For five years now Mel and Sue had been touted as being destined for the superstar heights of French and Saunders or Morecambe and Wise, but somehow it hadn't quite happened for them yet. They were both starting to regret leaving the safety of *Light Lunch*, but neither woman was a quitter and they had to believe that there was still time for them to hit the big time.

Their new show had played well-received limited dates in London already and now had a sell-out pre-Christmas run at The Arts Theatre in the West End to look forward to. They were also scheduled to tour with it on a very limited basis in early 2003.

Although her bank balance was getting low, Mel was reluctant to tear herself away from baby Florence, and proper touring would mean whole nights away. Sue understood and was – for the time being – happy to work around her best friend. Also she was mainly just glad to take her mind off her personal life.

Emotionally, Sue felt exposed after her recent *Big Brother* experience and had no idea what was going to happen as a result of it.

When Sue bought the Sunday papers two days after she was evicted from the *Big Brother* house, she couldn't believe the headlines. She was described as a 'dark force' amongst the celebs in the house, and there was even an insinuation that she had suffered some kind of mental breakdown.

'I only had a little sob because I was homesick,' she said incredulously when she read the papers. She told the *Evening Standard* a few days later: 'Certainly I was the anti-thesis of the bright bubbly blonde Page 3 girl. I thought my inclusion might have made for diversity, but its possible some housemates felt threatened by the fact that I read English at Cambridge.'

Ouch. But at least she was being honest. And there were more than a few heads nodding along with her as they read that edition of the newspaper. At first she believed that everything had gone exactly as she feared, and that revealing her sexuality had been a giant mistake.

'I went in the house because I thought it was time to get my personal life out in the open, once and for all,' she said in the same interview. 'Sadly, exactly what I had expected after being on *Big Brother* has happened; in one week I've gone from being one half of Mel and Sue to being a lesbian comic.'

But slowly, she began to see things differently and to feel that a weight had been lifted now that the truth was out.

'Then it was as if I'd mainlined Horlicks,' she told the *Daily Mail* a few years later. 'A wonderfully warm and relaxing feeling came over me. Having to come out to everyone individually is awful. It felt like a tidal wave of relief in a way. I'd just outed myself to eight million people and although that sounds awful, it wasn't. For every gay person, coming to terms with your sexuality is an incredibly intense and personal thing, so to then spend the rest of your life coming out is exhausting. That is what it is to be gay. You spend your life coming out to people. But for me, it was over in seconds. I said: "Like it or loathe it, this is who I am. I can't change it, and I won't be an apologist for it". And you know what? I've never had to say I'm gay since.'

Slowly, Sue began to untangle herself from the situation and see it for what it really was – the best thing that could have happened. She began to accept it – and herself too.

'For years I'd dissembled,' she reflected three years later. 'There were the references to partners, all gender non-specific; the gaps in personal history – and I was sick of it. It was so stressful. Perhaps that's one reason why I was miserable.'

She told *DIVA* magazine in 2011: 'In a way, my battle with being gay was more a battle with myself. I think it was seen as, "Oh, I've got a problem with telling people". But I just had a problem with myself. Every part of me – not just the gay part. Also the way I looked, spoke, dressed and interacted with people... whether I was stupid or whether people disliked me. I had a raft of issues, and that was just another one.'

Sue was also feeling the weight of her responsibility to other lesbians. When she came out, she didn't want to present them in general as being confused, emotional and having fractured senses of self. She didn't want to let them down by being a lesbian in the public eye and not really coping well with it.

'You want to give them a slice of something pure and good about being gay,' she said in the interview. 'You want to say, "I'm delighted". Thing is, I am delighted. But maybe then I didn't look as if I was.'

Sue began to receive a flood of letters from people who were struggling with their own sexuality. 'I would always answer those and would always be very candid about my own experiences,' she said in the same article. 'I would encourage people not necessarily to come out, but to do what they want with their lives.'

She also took the press opportunity to clear the air about her ex-girlfriend. The two women still cared about each other deeply and were working to forge a friendship now that they had decided not to be together any more.

They'd even been pictured walking Pickle together on Hampstead Heath, which led the mercurial celeb journalist Niki Waldegrave to ponder in the *Daily Star* 'Goss' column whether they could be in fact be reuniting.

'I'm grateful she respected my wishes not to talk about us while we were still together,' Sue told journalist Veronica Lee from *The Evening Standard*, before bravely admitting: 'But I accept that if you want a career in the media, a lot of that privacy has to go. Rhona had to be honest or she would have been branded a hypocrite. I was upset purely because I hadn't been brave enough to do it myself.'

She also made it clear in the article that the past few months had taught her a great deal about herself and how she had faced her issues: and it had even helped her understand the break-up a little better: 'Rhona has always been very open and honest about who and what she is and the fact that I wasn't, contributed to us breaking up,' she admitted.

'Rhona is on the record as saying that I am the love of her life. I have gone on record saying the same. I have great respect for the fact that she didn't capitalise on our relationship while I was in the house, because God knows the offers that were made.'

Sue had one final thing to tell *The Evening Standard* on the matter. 'I don't believe my private life is interesting, but now surely everybody knows what my sexuality is and I don't have to mention it again. Now perhaps I can just go back to being funny.'

That was all she wanted and with that in mind she led by example and forced herself to move on. She guested on *Graham Norton* with Mel to promote their new stand-up show and the duo even found time to indulge in a new passion: music.

Sue had learnt piano as a child and had a broad taste in music.

'Everyone needs something in their life to root them back down,' she told *The Herald* newspaper. 'To me, playing music is a way of de-stressing: I whack out some hardcore Chopin on the piano. On the guitar I'm very limited – basically only things involving the chords A, D and E. I like a lot of classical and I'll listen to the Dandy Warhols or the Doves. But I am approaching my mid-thirties so I'm always reaching for the Mozart CD.'

Next to Sue, Mel was a relative musical novice. So when they decided to form their own band – purely for fun – she was relegated to learning the drums. They called themselves The Leatherheads, a nod to the suburbs where Mel grew up, and admitted to have teenage-boy-type aspirations of appearing on *Top of the Pops*.

Mel's drum teacher was French and referred to her drum kit as 'the beast'. During an early lesson he asked her to show him what she could do, and Mel carefully banged out a basic drum rhythm. He then told her he was going to leave her alone for a bit with 'the beast'.

'Basically, he wanted her to experiment. Go a bit crazy,' Sue explained while telling the anecdote in 2003. 'So he went away for fifteen minutes, and when he came back Mel was still there going dunk dunk, cheeee. Dunk dunk, cheeee.'

Mel, also at the interview, squirmed uncomfortably in her seat.

'I felt really silly. I was just sitting there laughing to myself and thinking, what the hell am I meant to do with the beast?'

Sue gently laughed at her old pal. 'You have to straddle and ride it,' she said. 'Not go dunk dunk, cheeee.'

They were clearly not destined for *Top of the Pops*, but they did book themselves one gig – playing three songs in Mel's brother's living room for his fortieth birthday. It was very rock and roll. On the second song Mel lost control of one of her drumsticks. 'My hand went totally rigid,' she says. 'The stick was slipping out – but I kept on drumming.'

Needless to say, the band didn't last long.

As December ended and 2003 arrived, Sue must have been relieved to see the back of her annus horribilus. It had been an exhausting 12 months. But putting it all behind her, she now had something very interesting to look forward to. She and Mel had lined up some lucrative work for January, which would hopefully bring the public's focus back to their work and expose them to a whole new audience.

On 17 January, a number of British newspapers published the following snippet:

> *Comedy duo Mel Giedroyc and Sue Perkins are joining Channel 4 breakfast show* RI:SE. *They will have their own half-hour section of the programme when it is relaunched. Former 11 O'Clock Show host Iain Lee and Edith Bowman will host* RI:SE *until 8.30am, with Mel and Sue following them.*

Mel and Sue were heading back home, both in the sense that they were returning to Channel 4 and to their old roles of presenting a chat show together. But *RI:SE* would prove to be an epic challenge.

CHAPTER 13

RI:SE AND SHINE

'It's so nice to be talking to you when no one's watching...'
Sue Perkins, *RI:SE*

In January 2003, the unpopular breakfast show *RI:SE* was given a makeover and relaunched on Channel 4. After being in existence for only a year, a full-on rebrand may have seemed a bit premature, but this was the least of its creators' worries.

The simple problem was, no one was watching it. Even ancient children's classic Noddy was beating it in the ratings, and its producers had no idea how to turn round its ailing fortunes.

In the 1990s, breakfast television had been in its heyday, with seminal show *The Big Breakfast* regularly pulling in 2 million viewers every morning. But after its charismatic and entertaining presenter Chris Evans first cut down his days from five to three, and then left in 1994, it began a slow decline that led to the end of the once much-loved programme after a decade on air.

Its fate had been sealed when its poor and floundering coverage of the Twin Towers falling in 2001 left it looking childish and past its sell-by date. The BBC had extensive coverage and analysis of the tragic events, Sky News had access to American interviewees and up-to-the minute reports of the unfolding events, and even *GMTV* managed to keep somewhat abreast of the situation – by interviewing a never-ending roster of celebrities for their opinion on the shocking terrorist attack.

Channel 4 axed *The Big Breakfast* in March 2002 and it was replaced by *RI:SE* just a month later. The new show was markedly different from its predecessor.

Initially presented by Kirsty Gallacher, Mark Durden-Smith and Edith Bowman, it was a dull and indifferent mix of celebrity chat, sport and comedy and was too insipid to secure any kind of niche in the already overcrowded breakfast market.

The critics hated it.

Eight months later, the first series ended on a low and the people behind *RI:SE* had a lot of thinking to do about which direction to take the show, which by that point was struggling to hold on to a paltry 200,000 viewers.

They kept former MTV presenter Edith Bowman and released the rest of the presenting gang. And then they began to look around for new faces to join her.

Mel and Sue were by then concentrating on their latest tour, which was a mix of audience participation and sketches – familiar ground for the duo. They were masters of using the audience for their material: when one woman once shouted out that she'd be grateful if they could finish soon because they had a babysitter at home, the duo spent the rest of their time not only teasing her but delving into the abundant humour of family-life and its pitfalls. Things were also going well, critically.

But as Mel told Graham Norton on his eponymous show in

early January 2003, the tour dates were still limited because of baby Florence, so the duo had plenty of free time. So when the *RI:SE* team approached them with a nice fat deal to present a half-hour segment on the show every morning, they had been only too happy to sign on the dotted line.

They'd be interviewing guests and playing games for the final half-hour of the show, and since bosses had moved it from the distant Isleworth BSkyB studios to the much more central Whiteley's Shopping Centre in Bayswater, it wouldn't be much of a commute, either.

The *Daily Record* reported that they were being paid £200,000 each to save the show and was positive about the duo's arrival: 'At least this lot will be funny, especially Mel and Sue. And we know they can't be worse than the last lot.'

With a new line up in place – former *11 O'Clock Show* host Iain Lee was joining Bowman for the early shift – and a new location, the show unveiled its shiny revamp to great expectations on 20 January 2003.

It was clearly now almost a carbon copy of *The Big Breakfast*: the presenters sat as a couple in front of a set of French doors, and filming seemed a much more relaxed affair with lots of crew involvement. There were more light-hearted games and outside broadcasts, and also more competitions, which bosses were hoping would attract viewers away from rivals like *GMTV*.

Both Mel and Sue were looking forward to getting back to live TV, a national role and a bit of regularity. On weekdays, a car would arrive to pick them up at 6:30am, they'd have their hair and make-up done and then they'd go on air. They were back home by midday.

For the next few months, the duo settled into a routine. They both went home to their babies – Mel to Florence and Sue to Pickle – and despite not knowing how long the show would last, they were fairly content.

Mel's life was a whirl of family activities. Florence was now nearly a year old, so most of the rest of Mel's day was spent taking her to places like the park or the zoo, where she had begun to mimic the animals. She was happy with her new life.

Sue, still single, was enjoying hanging out with friends, cooking, writing and taking Pickle to Hampstead Heath. There, they mingled with the other dogs and dog-walkers, and discovered a whole new community.

'There is a collection of hilarious people up there,' she told Scotland's *The Herald* that year. 'I meet about twenty new people a day, plus the old familiar hardcore of about thirty. It's very funny, because you talk through the dogs. First of all you sex the other dog – basically look to see if it has nuts – then ask how old he or she is. Then you talk about behavioural problems and stuff like that, but somehow, through the animal, you've bonded with the human being.

'You learn the most extraordinary stuff. You actually get quite close to people. And there is a lot of sexual intrigue too – I'd be lying if I said there wasn't. There's a lot of checking-out goes on up there.

'Davina McCall once said that the best way to meet a husband was to go walking your dog in the park. I haven't met my future wife yet, but I have had five serious crushes in the past year. I find it very difficult to have crushes on people, so it's quite a big thing for me.'

But as peaceful as their home lives had now become, their work life was very much unstable. The generation who had grown up with – and were even willing to be late to work for – *The Big Breakfast*, were now all grown up, and the new generation just weren't tuning in to *RI:SE*.

Most of its target audience was now watching MTV or listening to the radio. The show's executive producer, Sebastian Scott, knew what he was up against: '*The Big Breakfast* started with only BBC1 and ITV as opposition, but we are up against cable, satellite and local radio stations spending unprecedented amounts of money to attract audiences,' he told *The Scotsman*. 'We're trying to pick up the rump of *The Big Breakfast* audience and attract a new generation who've never got into the habit of watching TV at breakfast time.'

Scott admitted that mistakes had been made when the show first started. 'It wasn't distinct enough. But remember that *GMTV* was a disaster when it launched,' he told the newspaper, with a faint air of desperation.

In March, just two months after Mel and Sue had joined the cast, the show actually recorded zero viewers for one day. By this time, Edith Bowman had left and been replaced by ex-*Big Brother* winner and inexperienced presenter Kate Lawler.

Mel and Sue soldiered on, making light of the appalling viewing figures by joking about their lack of viewers and generally being their bright and chirpy selves.

'Welcome to one hour of unmitigated hilarity that's been collapsed into twenty minutes of piffle, due to lack of talent – or very much interest,' Sue once said, opening one of their morning segments.

Despite the unease they must have felt at the instability of their roles, Mel and Sue made the best of the situation and there were some memorable moments on *RI:SE*. Like when they interviewed

Derren Brown and he offered to read Mel's mind. 'I feel like I'm in the way,' Sue said, leaning back so he could see Mel. 'It's how I've felt most of my career…'

He asked Mel to think of an event from her childhood and duly told her almost exactly what she was recalling. Mel looked suitably astounded.

'There was this big conker tree,' she explained, filling in the small gaps in the story, once the mind specialist had done his "magic".

'And I used to get the conkers and make conker furniture using little pins to make tables and chairs… '

'That's so weird,' teased Derren.

' …and my mum forbade me from doing it and I had a tantrum.'

It was a funny story, but Mel wasn't finished: 'She put me in the bath and showered me with cold water,' she went on, as Sue tried her best to cut her off.

'That's wrong, that's wrong, we mustn't talk about that now,' she said, drowning Mel out. 'There are laws! We must cease conversations about that, thank you,' she yelled as everyone in the studio laughed.

They were so at ease with each other – such talented pros – that it was a shame they were on such a sinking ship of a show. Naturally self-confident, with the ability to finish each other's sentences, the duo could banter pretty much without end.

When they once contributed to a documentary about the Kiefer Sutherland thriller series *24*, the producer asked them a question but had to politely cut them off when they were still answering it an hour later.

No one blamed any of the presenters – Mel, Sue, or Iain Lee –

for the dire performance of *RI:SE*, which was being described as the bastard offspring of everything that had ever gone before it.

'Any fool can show *Noddy* or *Blue Peter* repeats,' a spokesman told *The Herald*. 'But it's difficult to do something different in TV and at least this is an alternative.'

But the problem was, it wasn't different, and it wasn't an alternative that anyone really cared about. Commenting on the show's poor presenting team, *The Herald's* critic wrote:

> *They aren't responsible for the show's concept and are clearly trying to make it work. A glimmer of hope is the Mel Giedroyc and Sue Perkins segment at the end of the show that at least livens things up. But when an innocent remark by Perkins (a contestant on last year's* Celebrity Big Brother*) to winner Mark Owen – 'It's so nice to be talking to you when no one's watching' – gets the show's biggest laugh, it is in trouble.'*

Eventually, with no improvements in the ratings, the women admitted they had no idea what was going on – with the show or their rolling contracts. 'We don't know yet how long we're on for," Mel told the *Daily Record* 'We're like the YTS – we're working on a daily basis and they'll tell us if we're needed the next day. We've got our fingers crossed that we are going to make it through the next week.'

They knew that with *RI:SE's* future uncertain, they couldn't rely on it for a sustained source of income. So they continued to work on their stand-up together, with the intention of taking it to the Edinburgh Fringe in August.

In July, the duo were mysteriously missing from Britain's early morning screens and people must actually have been watching it then because their absence was definitely noted by journalists. Rumours began to fly.

The Mirror's celeb journalist Polly Graham wrote: 'Over in Z-list Land, everyone is beginning to wonder if Mel (Giedroyc) and Sue (Perkins) have been axed from *RI:SE*. Word is, the funny duo went on holiday for a week, and two weeks on still haven't returned.

'The talk at the Channel 4 show is the pair have been told they're no longer needed to host the final half-hour of the ailing show. Or perhaps they've had enough of the cringingly bad early-morning show.

'The girls joined in January in the umpteenth relaunch with new presenters Iain Lee and Edith Bowman. Now Edith's also gone the show's in the incapable hands of ex-*Big Brother* winner Kate Lawler and Iain. How long till it disappears, like its predecessor *The Big Breakfast*?'

Graham was right in that something had definitely happened. And she was definitely correct in her assertions that the show was in its final death throes. But she was wrong about the reason for Mel and Sue's absence: it was actually nothing to do with the show.

Mel was pregnant again.

'I can reveal why Mel and Sue have been mysteriously absent from Channel 4's dire morning show *RI:SE*,' scooped a *Daily Mail* columnist later that month. 'The duo have not, as widely thought, been sacked, but are missing because Mel Giedroyc is pregnant with her second child and suffering terrible morning sickness. A Channel 4 spokesman says: "Mel and Sue are a double act so that is why they are both not there. We're not sure when they will be back".'

A few days after the revelation, the duo were back at *RI:SE* and giving candid interviews to the press to promote their upcoming performance at the Edinburgh Fringe. They discussed the events of the past few years – Sue's coming out and Mel's motherhood – and revealed that, surprisingly, the public still didn't quite have a grasp on which one was Mel and which was Sue.

'The other day I got an e-mail from a newspaper that said they wanted to discuss with Sue issues about her baby and husband and to discuss with Mel issues about being gay,' Sue told *The Daily Mail*. 'I just looked at it and laughed. It doesn't really bother us, but you would think that after all this time people would probably have more of a grip.'

'Sometimes it does bug me,' admitted Mel in the same interview. 'But other times I find it quite amusing. I suppose it depends on what mood I am in. There are some people who just shout out, "Channel 4!" at us. That covers all the bases, really.'

Sue admitted that she sometimes felt it said something about the relationship between the two women: 'I find it kind of affirming that we are interchangeable, she said in the interview. 'We are a unit. If people shout, "Mel!" at me I just smile and walk on.'

Mel spoke about her excitement at adding to her and Ben's little family, and said that they couldn't wait for the Fringe so that they could finally have a lie-in. They were soon to take time off to travel up for Scotland and prepare for the show. But they didn't mention what was happening with their jobs, or say anything negative about *RI:SE* in general.

When they duly arrived in the Scottish capital at the end of the month, Sue gave an interview to the *Sunday Mail*. 'A week off is like getting your life back,' Sue said about not having to get up early for *RI:SE*. 'To be honest I don't wake up until after the show's finished. Come 9am, I'm zinging – right! I'm ready to tell some jokes!'

In the interview, she admitted that the early mornings were exhausting and being roused from bed at 5am was akin to waking the dead: 'The problem is, I still go to bed around midnight,' she explained. 'Mel's in bed by 8pm. That's why she looks about twelve and I look about 105.'

Journalist Steve Hendry, who conducted the interview, coaxed Sue into talking about their future on the show, writing that: 'They were brought in as part of a revamp to save the ailing show and while their presence hasn't quite managed that, they have avoided been tarnished by its failure.'

But Sue was unfailingly positive and wouldn't be swayed into saying something she could possibly regret. 'There's a lot of speculation about the show,' she said tactfully. 'If it does dry up we're not going to spiral into reclusive alcoholism. We'll do something else.'

She spoke about how excited she was to visit her new niece or nephew in nearby Glasgow, where her brother and his wife lived and were expecting a baby.

And she said how pleased she was to be back in Edinburgh, a city she was by now very familiar with. There were so many friends to catch up with and old haunts to revisit; it was going to be a good few weeks.

The comedy pair were still putting the finishing touches on their show, which would be performed at the Pleasance One, a good-sized venue. Like all their other stand-up shows, it would be only loosely planned and Sue admitted that she was under no illusions that it was going to be an easy experience.

'I think there will be a bit more pressure on us because people will think, "They've copped out, they sell bread and are sagging, yesterday's people",' she told Hendry. 'So we will have to do some work but that's good for us because we are the laziest double act in the western hemisphere.'

She described her and Mel's comedy process, which hadn't changed in over 10 years. 'We tend to be fairly last minute,' she explained to the same Scottish newspaper. 'There's no process, no artistry, it's just "Oh that's funny... " and then this incredible tension as you are about to go on stage and you realise, "We have no material".'

Something else that hadn't really changed was her self-effacing view of herself, her work and life in general. 'But we've managed to survive so far,' she added, thoughtfully. 'If it all ends tomorrow I'll still think, "Bloody hell how did we manage to get away with that?"'

The show was popular and the week-long stint was a sell-out. The reviews were great, with *The Guardian*'s Brian Logan calling them very 'likeable performers', and saying that their 'ad-libbed backchat' generated 'bigger laughs than the script'. This was no news to the duo's fans, who knew that they were coming to see Mel and Sue banter with each other, not an hour's worth of rigorously scripted material. It was their quick wit and easy friendship that made them the successful and popular comediennes they were.

As Logan surmised: 'Their enthusiastic following is thrilled to see the duo's spry, fun-poking relationship translated to the stage.' He went on: 'Which is just as well because Giedroyc and Perkins are very much subjects of their own show... Fun is had with Perkins' loathing of femininity, and of sincerity – which, "quite frankly, to me, is poison". The pregnant Giedroyc, faintly satirising her own girlishness, is the perfect counterpoint. And they do dressing up and funny voices with relish.'

But since, as a theatre critic Logan had to be even-handed, he did have one criticism – while he couldn't fault the women or their performing talent, he grumbled that: '... the performance outstrips the material. When they play themselves as ageing luvvies you savour the outré characterisation, but barely notice what they're talking about. With their skits on holiday reps and Hispanic soap operas, meanwhile, Mel and Sue stray onto the scorched earth of comedy terrain: nothing grows there. The pair are over-amplified in Pleasance One, but it's the substance of their comedy, not its volume, that should be more piercing.'

Logan made it sound like more of a criticism than it actually was. As he had said at the very beginning of his review: 'We're in the realm of proficient, comforting light-ent here and fair enough if that's what you're after.'

And for the most part, that is what people are after when they watch comedy. They want to be absorbed in a charismatic performance. They want to forget about everything else in their world for an hour or two. Quite simply, for the most part, they just want to laugh – and there were plenty of belly-shaking, gut-jiggling giggles and shrieking guffaws at the Pleasance One that week.

The Scotsman was similarly in two minds about the sold-out show. 'Mel and Sue are, despite now being national television stars, just as you might remember them from festivals past – jolly, likeable girls doing sub-studenty, actress-turned-comedienne, fluffier-than-funny sketches,' began its review. 'Of course now they have been touched by fame, reality TV, lesbianism and pregnancy. And it all goes into their show, much to the obvious gratification of a packed Pleasance venue.'

But then came the criticism, which like Logan's, couldn't quite be adequately put into words. 'Mel and Sue are a bit of a comedy conundrum. They are smart women, they are charismatic and they can do all the wig-and-a-funny-voice stuff as well as the next girlie double-act, but somehow their whole is less than the sum of their parts.

'There is nothing particularly wrong with the show, and the rest of the audience seemed to love it. Every reference to baking bread or being butch was greeted with laughter and applause. And, when microphones slip and the girls come off-script, we had some of the sharpest moments in the show.'

Also, just like Logan, *The Scotsman*'s reviewer had to admit that the show was well-loved by the audience. So whatever they and other reviewers felt about that enigmatic 'something' they believed was lacking, no one could deny that Mel and Sue's show was a hit with the most important critics of all – the paying customers who chose to go and watch it.

'To be "the show", performers need to kick a little comedy ass somewhere along the line,' added *The Scotsman*'s reviewer. 'I think Mel and Sue are fun to watch, super on a sofa and were so likeable in *Light Lunch*, but for me they are Delia Smith and I'm a Gordon Ramsay girl. But Delia is not doing too badly, so what do I know?'

CHAPTER 14

TIME TO CHANGE

'There was a time when it seemed to be very good for us as a duo.
At the moment there's not maybe a place for us on TV as there once was.'
Mel Giedroyc, *The Newcastle Journal*

Channel 4's *RI:SE* didn't last much longer after Mel and Sue returned from their successful expedition to Edinburgh and the Fringe.

In September that year, the channel's Director of Television, Tim Gardam, released a statement: 'Everyone involved has worked very hard to make a good and popular breakfast programme and there is no doubt it has improved in quality and content and is now a confident programme,' he said generously. 'But we have to reluctantly conclude that *RI:SE* is not going to grow a sufficient audience to justify it continuing into a third year.'

By now heavily pregnant, it made no real difference to Mel, who would have to stop work soon anyway. But it was yet another hiatus for the duo, whose careers were now beginning to drift.

Bored and out of work, Mel began to write a book documenting her pregnancy – initially more for herself than with any real intention of getting it published. She needed to keep her mind active because she was pretty much out of action physically for the last few months of gestation.

In February 2004, Mel gave birth to her second daughter, Vita. She and Ben were blissfully happy with their family, and though they weren't rich, they were definitely making ends meet.

They still had a huge mortgage on their beautiful five-bedroom home in Acton – which had the luxury of a 52-ft garden for the children but the money Mel had been receiving from the duo's ongoing Kingsmill advertising campaign had mainly been successfully bankrolling the family through her out-of-work periods. By now Ben was a freelance director and the husband and wife team shared parenting duties with each other and their flexible careers.

Mel and Sue's most recent Kingsmill advert had aired in mid-2002, as the latest addition to the company's 'fresh-thinking' campaign, which aimed to encapsulate the brand's 'fresh and modern approach' to bread advertising. It opened with Mel and Sue both working in a bakery, where a customer requests a loaf of their 'delicious sliced white'.

Sue says they've just baked a fresh batch, but hands over a Kingsmill Gold loaf from out back. They're rumbled when the company's delivery van pulls up so they rush comically to the door to disguise it.

It was another successful advert from agency Publicis, and board account director Lynn Avery said that Mel and Sue had been chosen for the latest campaign 'as they emulate freshness, energy and modernity, the values attributed to Kingsmill and its audience of modern mums with children.'

But by 2004, Kingsmill had clearly decided they wanted to try something new: Mel and Sue both received letters saying their services were no longer needed. It was a huge bombshell and one that would have extensive repercussions for both their lives.

They weren't the only stars being dropped by advertisers at the time either. Back in 2000, nearly every advert had had a big name backing the brand. While Mel and Sue were promoting Kingsmill, their old mentor Dawn French was doing the same for Terry's Chocolate Orange; Jamie Oliver was getting into bed with Sainsbury's; Griff Rhys Jones was inexplicably advertising Vauxhall cars; Ian Wright was glorifying a dreadful new dinner in a jar with the most catchily irritating theme tune, 'Chicken Tonight'; and even 1990s' iconic sitcom couple Neil Morrissey and Leslie Ash were getting in on the action for Homebase.

The market was saturated with big names lending their pulling power to big brands, and eventually it began to leave a sour taste in consumers' mouths. By 2003, the advertising industry was moving on, and rather than it being seen as cool to have a celeb feature in your ad, it simply made it look like they had run out of ideas.

The most iconic adverts of the next few years relied on ingenuity rather than recognisable faces and were better off for it – Whassup from Budweiser, Guinness's powerful Swimmer advert and Lynx's Lynx Effect to name just a few.

Kingsmill's next advertising campaign (the first without Mel and Sue for over five years) would hinge on one simple pun: Elvis Presley launching his own bakery in the UK – The King's Mill. Filmed in newsreel style and using a series of exceptional impersonators, it showed Presley arriving at Prestwick, Scotland, in 1960 before travelling to Uxbridge to found the bakery. The new slogan was: By appointment to 'The King'.

It was beautifully executed, but seemed an odd choice – using a man whose 10,000 calorie-a-day eating habit was ultimately responsible for his death to advertise a food brand that wished to be seen as healthy.

Jo Sykes, UK Marketing Director at Allied Bakeries, explained: 'Our campaign with Mel and Sue was very successful, but we felt it was time for a change. What better way to raise the profile of Kingsmill than using "The King" himself. We have always used tongue-in-cheek humour in our ads, and we hope that this new ad brings a smile to the faces of the great British public.'

It's telling that today, in most people's minds, memories of the Mel and Sue adverts surface more readily than the Elvis one.

Losing the Kingsmill campaign was very bad news for the pair. The adverts had been a very lucrative source of income, and effectively it had been very much funding their lives. Finding new work was of paramount importance, even if it was separately and however piecemeal.

Sue's earnings had plummeted by 65 per cent in the years following her coming out as a lesbian, and Kingsmill had definitely been a lifesaver as she'd tried to get her career back on track. For Mel it was particularly stressful: she was now mum to two very young children and so she had added responsibilities. Whereas in her twenties struggling for money meant sleeping on friends' sofas or going back home to Mum and Dad, she now had a huge house with an equally huge mortgage and two hungry mouths to feed. Not that she ever complained – they were the absolute light of her life.

'My kids are the best thing that ever happened to me,' she explained to *The Big Issue* soon after Vita's birth. 'I know that sounds flipping cheesy but its totally true. They just blew me away. They make everything worthwhile. They're so much fun and so interesting. It's such a bloody privilege.'

She also explained to the magazine how having Florence and now Vita had changed her perspective on pretty much everything. 'I remember looking at my first baby, just a few days old in her little basket, and I was suddenly very aware of my own mortality. I'd never thought about dying before. It's a weird one. It signalled my sudden going back to church: that fear of death, it made me go back to praying.'

Sue was also praying in 2004 – that Pickle wouldn't die. That year, her beloved pet fell gravely ill and for a while it was touch and go as to whether she would survive. Sitting up with her on one crucial night vigil, Sue was so distraught she made a promise.

'I'm not a practising Catholic,' she later explained to *The Scotsman*. 'I haven't been to Mass since I was ten, I haven't even seen the inside of a church in 25 years. But in that moment I made a pact with God.'

If Pickle lived, she bargained, Sue would give up the fags, a habit she'd been trying to kick for years. The sun rose, Pickle eventually recovered, and Perkins never smoked again.

Things were really changing for the comedy duo and it was around this time that they noticeably began working on separate projects in order to make ends meet.

Sue was a recurring and entertaining guest on *The Terry and Gaby Show*, a daytime chat show broadcast on Channel Five on weekday mornings. Her ex, Emma Kennedy was a movie reviewer on the show, so it was a fun programme to work on. But it was another dismal failure of a chat show, this time presented by Gaby

Roslin and Terry Wogan and created by Chris Evans' production company UMTV.

Now run by another Chris – Evans' former colleague Chris Gillett – the company has since become a resounding success. But back then *The Terry and Gaby Show* was hailed as yet another of the company's flops, although Evans himself made light of the show's failure.

It was much-hyped before its launch in 2003 and he'd publicly vowed to return to his former profession of selling fruit and veg if it failed. Four days after Sue's last appearance on the show, the final episode was aired, and it ended with a shot of Evans next to a market stall – called 'Chris's Fruit and Veg' – merrily chomping on an apple. He turned to the camera and good-naturedly said: 'Fuck it, we had a go, didn't we?'

Sue's voice was particularly in demand and she narrated a lot of documentaries, such as the fairly self-explanatory *The Twisted Lives of Contortionists* and *Carry on Calling*, a short film about the London Gay and Lesbian Switchboard.

She was also booked to read aloud a famous Oscar Wilde line for the 150th anniversary of the writer's birth, for the documentary *Happy Birthday Oscar Wilde*.

And she was team captain on the new late-night version of *Win, Lose or Draw*, a celeb game show inspired by the board game Pictionary.

The 11:30pm late-night show was a lot ruder than the gentle daytime programme, and had Liza Tarbuck as its presenter. And it had alcohol: lots of alcohol for its guests. Sue was perfect on the show, which had a full roster of celebs putting pen to paper for the competition, including Jo Guest, Gail Porter, Sarah Cawood and Sue's former *Big Brother* housemates Mark Owen and Les Dennis.

But other than this and a bit of extra radio work, Sue's schedule was pretty free, so she spent a lot of her time writing and walking on Hampstead Heath with Pickle. She'd met many new friends through her peaceful rambles, and it was around this time that she met Kate Williams, an attractive artist with a dog of her own. Slowly, their friendship would turn to something more.

Meanwhile, Mel had finished her pregnancy book and found that publishers were interested in it and by the end of the summer, Ebury Press had snapped up her manuscript, paid her an advance and published it under the title: *From Here to Maternity – one mother of a journey*. She gave numerous interviews to publicise the book, which was semi-autobiographical and took the form of a humorous pregnancy diary.

About that time she spoke to *The Newcastle Journal* about her working relationship with Sue, and gave the first hint of what was shortly – and probably inevitably – to come.

'You have to be realistic and take the opportunities that are out there,' she said carefully. 'There was a time when it seemed to be very good for us as a duo. At the moment there's not maybe a place for us on TV as there once was. There are loads more people coming up to fill the gap but I'm sure that will change and there'll be a niche for us again.'

But though it seemed obvious that they were definitely going to go their separate ways, Mel made it clear in the interview that she wasn't turning her back on working with Sue and revealed that, in fact, they were working on a new show together.

'I'll go round to Sue's house, we'll gossip solidly for two hours about everything under the sun, then we'll work for half-an-hour and then I'll go. It's shambolic. Our organisational skills are legendarily bad.'

She also discussed the difficulties of being a working mother, especially a working mother in show business, where popularity waxes and wanes in the blink of an eye: 'I feel very torn because I adore my kids and I know this time is so precious,' she told *The Journal.* 'I would hate to get to the stage where I thought I'd missed the first four years of their lives, but in this business you've got to keep your hand in, otherwise you're forgotten.'

Mel was right. Money was getting ever tighter and work was increasingly scarce. The next few years would be a struggle. And whatever new show she was referring to in the interview, it never materialised.

The following year Sue confirmed that the duo were splitting.

CHAPTER 15

GOING SOLO

'We always wrote separately anyway and particularly in the
last few years because of the practicalities of Mel being a mum.
I had no wish to see her writing and breast-feeding.'
Sue Perkins, *The Sunday Mail*

By 2005, Sue was finally ready for a solo career. After years struggling with a secret but crippling lack of confidence, she was finally getting to the stage where she was at peace with herself and felt able to face the spotlight alone.

And the first step was communicating that to the press, who wanted to know when Mel and Sue would be back on British TV screens.

'In the middle of all that fun,' she revealed to *The Daily Telegraph*, while describing the *Light Lunch* years, 'working with somebody I adored, I was covering up the fact that I didn't feel like a real person. I used to think, why would I go and talk about myself for an hour and who would be interested anyway?'

Sue had now confronted most of her issues head-on – and often publicly. Her personal life was feeling more settled and things with her new girlfriend Kate were going well. She was beginning to think about children again and was feeling an urge to settle down. Partly it was due to her age.

'In my twenties and thirties I did all those panel shows, and came away from them feeling cowed and bullied, and I'd beat myself up afterwards about how I'd barely said a word,' she said to the *Daily Mail*, talking about moments like when she went on *Have I Got News For You*.

'I'd feel real shame, to the point where I was afraid to speak to anyone, or answer the phone,' she added. 'But that's changed. Maybe it's about growing older and accepting yourself. The idea I'd behave like that now is ridiculous.'

And with work for the duo now scarce, she'd come to the conclusion that it was time to make her own way in the world for a while. 'Mel is married with two kids now and less work is coming in for us as a double act,' she told the *Daily Mirror*, before making it clear that there was no question that the pair would work together again. 'Working together has always been our favourite thing and it is where our hearts lie.' But she also knew she had to be realistic.

'We are in our mid-30s, we both have to work and can't sit about waiting for work to come through the door,' she explained to the *Sunday Mail*. 'And, at some point in any relationship, you do want to go off and explore different things. Mel has her family and different priorities but we don't really make much distinction between our friendship and our working lives. We're both supportive of our individual stuff and hopefully next year we will be back together.'

Sue began working on her very first solo stand-up show and felt a new sense of ambition burn inside her. Things would be very different now, but she was excited about what the future would bring.

Meanwhile, Mel was also branching out. After also deciding on a 'dramatic' change, she went back to her roots and began auditioning for acting roles. It wasn't long before she landed the part of Sue Chandler, Ardal O'Hanlon's wife in the new Ben Elton comedy drama *Blessed*. Filming began in January 2005.

It had been a decade since Elton's last BBC1 hit, *The Thin Blue Line*, and since then he had kept himself busy writing a series of very popular West End musicals.

Blessed signalled his return to sitcoms, and was greatly anticipated by both the media and the public.

It was different to anything he'd done before – a domestic drama about a married couple struggling to bring up their babies, in stark contrast to their annoyingly perfect neighbours.

The eight-episode first series was an uneasy watch. It had high production values and felt like it should have been successful, but there was something missing and it felt dated and unadventurous.

Critic Jim Shelley from *The Daily Mail* was hugely unimpressed: 'Throughout, *Blessed* had nothing to say about parenthood that isn't already a ludicrous, empty stereotype. In a year of brilliant British comedies such as *Little Britain*, *Extras*, *The Thick of It*, *People Like Us*, *Help*, and *Nathan Barley*, it was also horribly old-fashioned.

'The longer *Blessed* went on, the more my feelings towards Ben Elton's kids moved from indifference to hate for inspiring such twaddle. Couldn't they be taken into care to stop any further crimes against comedy?'

In 2013, the *Metro* retrospectively featured it in its list of top ten worst sitcoms, writing that much of the blame lay with the show's main star, O'Hanlon, and his 'inability to deliver Elton's trademark rants in quite the same way as Elton himself'.

It was a rare misstep for the comedy king, and a crying shame for Mel, who deserved and needed a hit. Unsurprisingly, a second series wasn't commissioned.

In March, while Sue was testing out her new show material on Pickle – 'she usually falls asleep, which is a good gauge of how the audience will respond' – Mel appeared on *The Games*, a Channel 4 reality TV series that pitted 10 celebrities against each other in Olympic-style events such as weight-lifting, gymnastics, speed skating and diving. At the end of the nine-day competition the contestants with the most points were awarded gold, silver or bronze medals.

Presented by Jamie Theakston and Jayne Middlemiss, the show was filmed in Sheffield and involved months of gruelling training. It must have been an interesting experience, because during training, the celebs were put through their paces by world-class sporting experts such as Colin Jackson and Fatima Whitbread before competing in the event.

Mel's fellow contestants on what was season three of the show included Lisa Maffia, Kirsty Gallacher, Craig Charles and Chesney Hawkes. Mel had a lot of fun preparing for and filming the contest, but she didn't win any medals and by the middle of the year she was back looking for work again. And aside from appearing on two episodes of *Heaven and Earth* with Gloria Hunniford in the autumn, work continued to be very scarce. It was a stressful time.

In late July 2005, Sue travelled to the Edinburgh Fringe and prepared to perform her new one-woman show, *Spectacle Wearer of the Year 2006*. In contrast to Mel, she was in a good place. She was well and truly in love with Kate and had even welcomed a new family member into her and Pickle's lives: just as she was revelling in having a new companion, so was Pickle, who now had Parker, another beagle, to play with.

By now, Pickle was calming down a little, much like her owner. 'Having a dog just stops the mania,' she reflected to *The Scotsman* in the run-up to her first performance. 'Pickle taught me how to relax, and I never used to do that. I had a lot of nervous energy, but I'm not like that anymore. Now I sit down and she comes and sits with me. At the end of the day, I don't have to be rushing around doing things all the time. I can just stay in with my pets.

'Parker rules the roost. Pickle is the pleasure model. She eats, sleeps and tries to have sex with other dogs. She's such a tart!'

It was clear that Sue was growing more and more broody, something that she was not very convincing at trying to hide. She was becoming very keen on the idea of being a mother, but obviously knew that for her, having children would much more complicated than it had been for her pal Mel, whose children she adored.

She had been making excuses for not having them for a few years now, because it was less painful than admitting the complexity of her desires to herself.

'I always say "I'm very busy, I've got a show here, I really need to write, I don't have the time",' she told *Scotland on Sunday* that summer. 'But I've thought about adopting and I know a couple of blokes who would make brilliant dads. It's a cruel trick that you get these biological nudges, because they don't always occur at the most convenient times, and for me they don't occur in a convenient sexuality either. But I do think about it, probably more than I admit.'

It was the logistics of being a gay parent that Sue was mostly grappling with.

'Who has it?' she asked poignantly in the same article, talking about pregnancy in a lesbian relationship. 'Do you both have one? It's going to take some time for me to get my brain around the ethics of it all. Not whether I think it's right or not, but how best to do it. It's a big responsibility. It's enough of a responsibility for a straight couple to bring up a child, but for me, I think, will that child get bullied, will it feel weird, how will I find the words to communicate the situation?'

They were valid concerns and ones that Sue would be consumed by for many years to come.

'But I'd still love to,' she added wistfully.

Having a child would also involve being in a stable and long-term relationship, and Sue was only in the very beginning stages with Kate. She was still cautious about naming her new girlfriend, but she was beginning to refer to her in the media in glowing terms.

'She's a very calm, lovely and grown-up person,' she told *The Scotsman*. 'She's much more grounded. I'm like a balloon that's burst. It's a good balance.'

The pair hadn't discussed moving in together yet, but Sue was positive enough about the relationship to be discussing both it and her sexuality with journalists – a far cry from a few years before when she was almost in hiding from the media over both issues.

'When we met we were friends and things developed from there,' she told the Scottish newspaper. 'Everyone wants crash, bang, wallop, but I mistrust sudden jolts of emotion.'

She was also confident enough to speak about her feelings on gay marriage: she was very pro them on a legal level and felt for example that it was a terrible oversight when the state failed to recognise the rights of gay couples in long-term partnerships when one of them died. But she wasn't interested in tying the knot herself.

'For myself, I hate the idea of a gay wedding,' she said in the same interview with *The Scotsman*. '"Oh, here comes the bride! And here comes the other one!" Awful. A couple of women in meringue dresses? I'd just die of embarrassment.'

This new Sue Perkins seemed confident and thriving, excited about her new show and brimming with enthusiasm for the future. She was nervous about her new solo venture, though, as anyone would be, but was full of ideas for the first time in a long while and had a new fire in her belly – as was very apparent in the interview:

'I feel a bit nervous. When you come from being in a double act, you don't want to go solo only to find out it wasn't you people came to see,' she joked. 'I can't imagine anything worse, but at the same time it would be quite funny. It's quite scary in that I'm used to somebody else being there with me and the stage seems a big space to fill – and there's nobody to help you out if things go wrong.'

But doing the new show was partly a way of proving something to herself. 'I think I want to prove I can tell jokes,' she mused to journalist Steven Hendry in *The Sunday Mail*. 'I want to be seen as a comic. Some of the things I've done on TV kind of detract from that. I'll always be grateful to TV because it's great money, but there are times when doing things like the Kingsmill Bread adverts – it pays the mortgage but I don't want the legacy on my tombstone to read, "Here lies someone who sold millions of loaves of white bread".'

For Sue, stand-up was the zenith of live entertainment, and after having always had Mel to rely on and riff off she wanted to know that she could be funny solo, too. Not forever though, as she was adamant that the 15-year partnership with Mel would resurface sooner rather than later.

There would be a huge part of her that would miss Mel's company in the capital. 'Where I will miss her is before and afterwards, going through all the little rituals and games and anecdotes we used to do and tell to keep us going,' she said in the *Sunday Mail* interview, reminiscing about their past Fringe experiences. 'It's a great way to earn a living but there are moments of stress, especially just before you go on... and Mel was awful for going to the toilet just before we went on. She would destroy porcelain around the country.'

Sue was secretly hoping that Mel would see the show and want to work on something for next year's Fringe. But it would be two years before Mel returned to perform in Edinburgh, and even then it wouldn't be with Sue.

Sue's new Fringe show *Spectacle Wearer of the Year 2006* was performed at The Pleasance Courtyard, and was a mixture of personal anecdotes, stories and observations.

It would not only be the first time she was going solo in Edinburgh, but the first time she'd done a full month-long run at the festival since 1999. She was anticipating the highs, lows and utter exhaustion that came with the intense performing schedule, and she was looking forward to it.

She would be surrounded by a lot of her comedy mates, like Richard Herring and Stewart Lee, who were also performing at The Pleasance, and would get the chance to take the dogs to visit her brother's family in Perth too, which she was excited about.

The month-long run began and Sue quickly proved what she had set out to achieve: that she could perform alone, on the live stage, and that she was a more than capable stand-up comic.

The premiere comedy website *Chortle* commented that she definitely passed her comedian's MOT at the first attempt, and described her as 'an engaging, wryly self-deprecating raconteur with a light but sure touch'. They praised her elegant prose, citing as an example her throwaway line describing tuna as 'brainless blocks of protein that float towards canning factories'.

'It may be only mildly amusing but it's a taut, efficient and very descriptive phrase,' said *Chortle*. 'Twenty-four hours later you might be hard-pressed to remember any of it [the show] but with Sue it's more about going along for a jolly ride... there's an air of professionalism that pervades every aspect of her show. Never once do you feel as if you're not in a safe pair of hands, even if you're equally unlikely to think you're in the presence of the next all-conquering comedy genius. But "reliably amusing" is still a surprisingly scarce attribute in comedy, so it's still worth celebrating.'

As the month went on, Sue felt more and more comfortable being alone on the small Pleasance stage, and was excited to see a packed audience waiting for her every single night.

'It was strange at first being up there without Mel,' she admitted to one journalist from *The Coventry Evening Telegraph*. 'But I started having a discussion with the audience getting them involved as if I was talking to Mel and asking them things and some of them have absolutely brilliant things to tell. There are absolutely mad people out there,' she enthused.

It was clear that Sue was happy, content, and proud of what she had so far achieved as a solo performer. It was the start of what would be a successful solo few years for that half of Mel and Sue.

CHAPTER 16

ANYTHING BUT DISAPPOINTING

*'It would be foolhardy for me to be confident about work.
I'm in an industry where most people are unemployed at any given
time, and I'm very lucky not to be one of them.'*
Sue Perkins, *DIVA*

After such an enjoyable Fringe run, Sue felt confident enough to take her show on tour. She spent a bit of time tweaking it, changing it, and introducing new material, and even set herself the challenge of ad-libbing the first 10 minutes of every show.

She was flexing her solo muscles and seeing what she could do and how she could do it. And it turned out that the answers were: 'quite a lot really' and 'exceptionally well'.

She described it as an 'old person's tour', because it wasn't as intensive as most. 'Someone like Dara O'Briain will do 60 dates in 60 days. I'm doing 60 gigs spread over an entire year,' she told *Time Out* in May 2006.

By then she felt that her stand-up techniques were improving and that she had learnt how to develop her routine. 'It's come slowly,' she said humbly to the magazine, 'I'm very impatient. I kept feeling that I wasn't good enough. Now at least I feel better inside my own skin. I've learnt how to play with each bit, to enjoy expanding on it. To get used to the stage being mine.'

And because of the sporadic tour dates, Sue had time to fit in plenty of the other work that came her way that year, so it was the perfect scenario. She recorded a few radio shows, guest-starred on *8 out of Ten Cats* and *The Wright Stuff*, popped up a number of times on the very short-lived Channel 4 game show *Back in the Day* and appeared as a talking head on a number of documentaries, including *Girls Who Do Comedy* and *50 Most Shocking Comedy Moments*.

She also embedded herself in the public consciousness by appearing on two very different competitive shows: *Showbiz Poker* and *Celebrity Masterchef*. Not being a very competitive person at heart, they were both very new challenges for the gentle and studious comic.

She initially took part in *Showbiz Poker*, a televised celebrity poker tournament, as a favour to a friend. She had never played the card game before, but to the astonishment of everyone around her, she just kept winning her games, even beating veteran footballer and poker pro Teddy Sheringham along the way.

'I kept getting through, all the way to the Grand Final,' she explained to one bemused journalist from *Time Out* in May when the tournament was over and she'd finally lost. 'Teddy was a nice guy and a real card player. I was riddled with guilt. It just shows how far you can get with a go-getting attitude. If you're a novice you don't feel so inhibited. You're not preoccupied with the subtleties of the game.'

Next she took part in another showbiz competition – and one where you equally need a good poker face – the BBC's *Celebrity Masterchef*. In her heat she competed against Toyah Wilcox and

Kristian Digby, over three rounds: an Invention Test, Pressure Test and Final Test.

Sue had had a very late foodie education, because as she herself admitted, her staple diet growing up was – though well-executed – unexotic.

'I've been cooking since I was four,' she told the *Daily Mail* during filming. 'My rock buns were tooth-breakers; my mum held them in her cheek for hours. We always ate together as a family. It wasn't idyllic – the television was always turned towards the table – but Mum is a good cook. There was lots of meat and potatoes, and we always had tinned peaches with Ideal milk.

'When pasta arrived in Croydon, it was exotic – and our mince and potatoes became lasagne. I ate my first avocado when I was twenty.'

But despite her modesty, she had spent years on *Light Lunch* watching celebrity chefs knock up stunning meals in the show's kitchen, and she had always enjoyed cooking for her friends at home. Mel always claimed she was a talented chef too.

In the first round, the Invention Test, Sue was a Tasmanian devil in the kitchen – a whirlwind of mess and flamboyance. 'Whenever I enjoy something I make a dreadful mess,' she admitted.

There were splatter marks up the wall, herb flecks over the sparkling glasses and hundreds of ingredients pulled out of the cupboards. Judge John Torode watched her work with amazement, first impressed at her imagination and then worried as she slowly got more and more carried away with the excitement of it all.

Eventually she mistook an orange for a grapefruit and served the judges a sardine and tomato salad with orange dressing – not a winner, unfortunately. For The Pressure Test, the trio headed to London restaurant Addendum to work a real lunchtime service.

They were supervised by the stern-but-fair chef Tom Ilic, who said that under no circumstances would he be letting anything substandard leave his kitchen.

Sue was in charge of the seafood special, Monkfish in a seafood and spring vegetable broth. She remained calm in the heat and stress of the kitchen, focused on her dish. She was a lot cleaner and tidier than she had been during the Invention Test, and Illic was impressed. 'It sings spring to me,' he told her after tasting it. It was high praise, and at least she didn't nearly burn the kitchen down like Kristian. It was an intense two hours and in the end it was Toyah who came out just ahead of her two rivals.

Finally, Sue had to cook a main course and dessert for the judges – Torode and his co-presenter Gregg Wallace. She chose starter and main, and went for a complicated looking crab salad to start and a simple roasted whole mackerel for the main event.

'The mackerel was delicious,' said Torode. 'Sue produced us two individual dishes which were both coherent and full-flavoured.'

'The crab was okay,' said Wallace, a bit hesitantly. 'I'm not sure she knows quite when to leave alone.'

Sue didn't progress to the quarter-finals, but she gave a great account of herself on the show. John Torode was particularly impressed by Sue's relaxed attitude and singled her out for praise in an interview he later gave to the *Daily Mail*. 'Sue Perkins was a really good natural cook,' he said. 'I'd go to dinner at Sue's house any day of the week. She's fun, she's a laugh and there's nothing pretentious. And her orange and sardines – not a good combination – was still better than squid and redcurrants [later contestant Linda Barker's shocker of a combination].'

Sue's stand-up tour continued to make its slow but successful progress around the country. It was a good snapshot of where she was in her life – like a new solo starting point, a new self-introduction to the world. And it was a successful one. So she began to prepare another Fringe show for the summer, and in line with her self-effacing personality she called it *The Disappointing Second Show*.

Sue was definitely happy in her professional life. 'I've just developed a healthier attitude towards work,' she said to *DIVA* magazine half way through the year. 'I love mine. It's the most interesting job in the world, and the people are the most hilarious and brilliant.'

But however good her life was workwise, she was positively blissful in her personal life. After over a year as a couple, she and Kate were ready to move in together. Sue was overjoyed and didn't care who knew it. 'I tell you, I'm boxing above my weight there,' she revealed in the same *DIVA* interview. 'She's gorgeous.'

Gone were the days of keeping everything locked away and hidden from the public. She was still a private person and that would never change, but she now didn't shy away from answering questions about her sexuality or her girlfriend.

It was a refreshing change and a big step for the sensitive comic. But moving in together was an even bigger step than it normally would have been: because both she and Kate were planning on leaving London behind altogether.

On holiday a few years earlier, Sue had fallen in love with Cornwall, even shedding a few discreet tears when she left to return to London. But they obviously weren't just regular post-holiday blues because now she was actually moving there with Kate, and it wasn't difficult to see why: with plenty of space for the dogs and a special kind of natural beauty it was an idyllic place to live.

She'd found the perfect smallholding at the very tip of the county, near Penzance, for £500,000 – a three-bedroom home with three acres of land and a few outbuildings. The slower pace of life would fit right into Sue's new, more laid-back attitude to life, and it was still commutable to London by car for any work that came her way.

Over the next few years she would take her time renovating the eighteenth-century farmhouse and lovingly planting her own vegetables in the garden. There was plenty of room for Kate to store her artist supplies, and the rural beauty would be a special kind of inspiration for both women's creative output.

Sue and Kate started their new life in the countryside just weeks before the Edinburgh August Fringe. 'I go home and it all stops,' she told *DIVA* magazine, describing her new lifestyle. 'I don't take work with me. I enter this parallel life where everything is open, farmers mow the fields, you wave at your neighbours, you walk the dogs and you think about writing a novel – but you never do because you're so utterly paranoid it might not be a work of genius. Instead, it will be something despicably shoddy and mediocre. It's going to be chick-lit, whatever you try to do!'

Sue's whole world was now filled with a romantic air of contentment and she could only hope it would last forever. 'I led a very adrenalised, interior life in London,' she said in the same interview. 'I wanted to try an alternative way of living.' Moving to Cornwall was certainly that.

With her new life beginning and boxes still to unpack, Sue left for Edinburgh and the 2006 Fringe festival – where her second month-long show was once more destined to be a sell-out.

The Disappointing Second Show was more polished and scripted than her first solo show – an accomplishment in itself, considering

Sue's usual more ad hoc approach to comedy, but not something that everyone agreed made the show better.

Solo stand-up comedy was still a new experience for her and Sue saw it as a learning process. She had learned a lot during her first solo venture and would learn yet more this time around.

'I made a lot of mistakes and people were kind enough to keep supporting me,' she told *The York Press*. 'I'm still very green and very raw at it, but feel this show represents a real leap in my ability.'

The title of the show itself was a self-deprecating gift to the critics, of which she was sure there would be many. 'They can just lift the title for their review,' she said, wryly to the same paper.

But the show's theme was disappointment too, so the title wasn't all about preparing her audience for the worst. 'The theme of this show is not pessimism,' she explained to one journalist from *The Liverpool Daily Post*. 'It's about laughing at the relationship between expectation and disappointment. As soon as you're born, you start to fail to meet the expectations of your parents or your own expectations.'

The show was observational and very personal – Sue joked about family, being brought up a Catholic, being useless at technology and the expectations of the older generation. She had also gleaned a lot of material from her 'homophobic grandmother', now that she could finally joke about the 98-year-old's disapproval, which she had never mentioned before.

'I have to deal with her prejudice which is bellowed down the old people's home, and that she doesn't approve of me particularly but keeps forgetting, and I keep having to remind her that I'm not married,' she explained to *The York Press*. 'It can happen about four or five times an afternoon.'

It was still such early days in her solo career and she still had moments when she couldn't quite believe how far she'd come. 'When Mel and I were working together, if someone had suggested me going on my own into a darkened room full of strangers, I would have run a mile,' she told *The Daily Telegraph*.

But what was most important about the show was that her new-found openness, drive and ambition to overcome personal hurdles were all signs of her current contentment with life, which was obvious in her more confident demeanour on stage.

'I don't think I could do a show about disappointment and make jokes about it if I weren't content,' she told *The York Press*. 'So yeah, I think I'm in one of my most comfortable stages of my life. Now I think I know myself and I can finally do stand-up, which is so exposing.'

The reviews were – in general – good and the audience loved it, but there were some criticisms, which was inevitable. Dominic Maxwell at *The Times* wrote: 'It's called *The Disappointing Second Show* and I wish I could avoid the put-down that the title self-mockingly invites. But while Sue Perkins is a bright and confident performer, her second solo stand-up show is indeed disappointingly ordinary.'

His problem was that it lacked the spark of her usual improvisation. While Sue had worked hard on scripting this new show, he felt that her greatest talent lay in interacting with her audience, using her sharp and speedy comebacks: 'Some of the best moments in this 90-minute show are when she trusts her wits, dealing deftly with some attention-seekers in the crowd.'

And he also felt that, without Mel, Sue's sketches lacked a little energy. 'When she plays characters, too — particularly her 98-year-old Jewish granny — she exudes the star quality that she showed in her long-time double act with Mel Giedroyc.'

Above: FIRST TIME ROUND: The duo became 90s icons after *Late Lunch* made them stars – before life took them in different directions. (*©REX/ITV*)

Below: LARKING ABOUT: The pair have been best friends since university and see each other as family. (*©REX*)

I KNOW HER SO WELL: As Elaine Paige and Barbara Dickson on a celeb special of *Stars in their Eyes* in 2002.

(©*REX/ITV*)

Above: BRIEF ENCOUNTER: After *Late Lunch*, Mel and Sue presented the popular but short-lived panel show *Casting Couch* in 1999 – here they are with guests Amanda Holden and Pauline McLynn. (©*REX/ITV*)

Below: BEST FORGOTTEN: After the pals went their separate ways, Mel teamed up with Richard Hammond for his *5 O'Clock Show*. It was not a critical success.

(©*REX/ITV*)

Left: DETERMINED: Owning the floor in the gymnastics section of ITV's *The Games*. Mel went through months of gruelling training before taking part in the intense challenge in 2005.

(©*Getty Images*)

Right: DIVERSE TALENTS: Sue's emotional journey to the top included winning the BBC's celebrity conducting competition *Maestro*. The sensitive comic (*pictured here with fellow contestant Jane Asher*) went on to conduct the BBC Concert Orchestra at the Proms, in front of 30,000 people.

(©*REX*)

Above: TAKING THE STAGE: Channelling her inner-Lady Gaga, Mel took on the role of the wicked stepmother, Ms. Hardup, in a 2012 production of *Cinderella*. (©*REX*)

Below: HIDDEN LOVE: Sue dated comedienne Rhona Cameron for years without revealing her sexuality to the public. (©*Getty Images*)

BAKE OFF MAGIC: Mel and Sue pose on the red carpet for the show that has catapulted them to fame, *The Great British Bake Off*.   (©*Karwei Tang/WireImage/Getty Images*)

Above: OUT AND PROUD: After revealing her sexuality on Big Brother in 2002, Sue became something of a gay role model. Here she is raising awareness of homophobic bullying in schools, with the founder of Diversity Role Models, Suran Dickson (*left*).

(*©Getty Images*)

Left: TREADING THE BOARDS: Thespian Mel in *New Boy* with young actor Nicholas Hoult. While the critics loved her performance, the play itself was panned. (*©Getty Images*)

Above: PLAUDITS: Celebrating their first well deserved BAFTA with the rest of the *Bake Off* family - the show won the prestigious Best Feature award in 2012 and 2013.

(©*Getty Images*)

Below: HANDS OFF: The *Bake Off* has enjoyed great success, thanks in no small part to Mel and Sue's playful chemistry with judges Mary Berry (*pictured left*) and Paul Hollywood.

(©*REX/Stephen Butler/BAFTA*)

But Maxwell could also see her comedy qualities shining through: 'She can time a line, she can hold a stage, she's got a black belt in endearing self-effacement. And when Perkins lets herself off the observational leash, some of her more fanciful ideas are distinctive too. But it's the stuff about her own life that hints at what this very bright comic is capable of.'

She was learning and growing and constructive criticism was well received. And since it was a popular show, at the end of the month, Sue took it on a leisurely tour around the country, just as she had with *Spectacle Wearer of the Year 2006*.

It was sweetly telling though, that throughout the two shows, at each performance, Sue always stood to the left of the stage – as if there was an invisible line that she couldn't cross.

Mel's line.

'It's true,' Sue told *Time Out*. 'A friend recorded a show of mine and when I saw the tape I realised that I never crossed that imaginary dividing line, not once. It sounds weird, but I don't yet feel like it's my space to own… There's a zone that's kept free out of respect. There's a space that isn't my territory.'

It was comforting to the duo's fans, who still hoped one day to see them back together again, but somehow feared that their split was permanent. 'It's not,' Sue insisted in the same interview. 'I love being with her. But we have to go where the work is.'

And the work still wasn't to be found together, unfortunately.

CHAPTER 17

GOING GA GA

'When you've had a baby in showbiz, people think you've died...'
Mel Giedroyc, *The Daily Mail*

J ust like Sue, Mel started 2006 heading in a totally new direction – when she began working with a new comedy partner, in the form of *Top Gear*'s Richard Hammond.

In January, she joined forces with the pint-sized star to co-present ITV's new weekday programme, *The 5 O'Clock Show*. She beat off stiff competition to land the job on the show, which had been designed to replace the popular *Paul O'Grady Show*, which had recently moved to Channel 4.

It was 60 minutes long and featured a variety of segments on both popular and unusual topics. For example, the duo tested out contemporary inventions like the unstainable suit or unbreakable crockery, and even gave unknown wannabe comics a minute on stage to prove how funny they were.

It was a melting pot of unique ideas, none of which had any real link between them, so viewers never really knew what was coming next. In one regular slot, Hammond attempted to find the exact centre of Britain, while in another Martin Lewis dolled out money-saving tips. Mel and Richard regularly interviewed the contestants and judges of that year's *Dancing on Ice*, Russell Watson performed operatic football chants and Sara Cox held ferret races.

It was wacky, innovative and apart from the *Dancing on Ice* segments, which were obviously put in because they had to be (the programme was on the same channel, hence the plug), really fun. Which made the absolute panning it got by the critics a complete surprise. They reviled it.

Come join us as we dance over the corpse of weekday afternoon television [read one particularly nasty review on the website IMDB]. *Witness the carnage left over by Paul O'Grady's sudden defection to Channel 4! Notice the absence of warmth and humour from the schedule after his untimely departure! Whatever will ITV do with the slot now? Show more repeats? Invent a new soap opera? Have an extended news bulletin? Nope, they decide to launch a new chat show! One with a 'rising star' you know, that bloke from* Top Gear, *and the non-lesbian from the duo who used to present* Light Lunch. *Then, add lots of useless gadgets for them to review, produce stupid games they play with the visibly-bored audience and line up tons of interviews with D-listers who'll be stacking the shelves at Asda a year from now and what have you got? A load of old pants, that's what.*

But families and teenagers loved it. A healthy dose of light-hearted fun, it was so far removed from the usual dreary chat show offerings that it became the talk of the school gates – according to some fans who defended it on the IMDB message board:

I'm amazed people slated this show [wrote one]. *I thought it was terrific and so did the vast majority of kids at school according to my kids. It was wacky, funny and unpretentious.*

Mel and Richard had us in stitches everyday. I despair. I thought for certain that it was going to sound the death knell of the dreary, self-congratulatory, po-faced Richard and Judy.

Everyday at the school gates the children's talk was all of what was on the 5 O'Clock Show *the previous evening. I really cannot see what there was about this show that anyone could find to dislike.*

One 13-year-old fan added: 'I happen to love this show its a load of laughs plus when I've had a bad day at school I like to just sit down and watch some good television like *Deal or no Deal* and the *5 O'Clock Show* not rubbish shows like *Richard and Judy!*'

After just one season, lasting six weeks and 30 episodes, the show disappeared into the TV ether. It was a strange phenomenon. Most shows got criticised for not being creative or innovative enough. Then one came along that was just that and it still wasn't good enough. Maybe it should have been more firmly targeted towards the younger generation, with the very adult-looking audience replaced by teens, because they were certainly the ones who mourned the show when it ended in February of the same year. 'I'll miss it when it ends tomorrow,' wrote one online fan, sadly.

Whatever the reason, for Mel it must have been very

disappointing. It could have been the perfect job for her – a family show, London-based regular hours. Instead she was back to searching for whatever would come next.

Mel's second book was published in the summer: *Going Ga Ga – is there life after birth?* Picking up from where her first book left off, it was a humorous account of Mel's early days as a mum, and was written in the same semi-fictional style. It captured all the madness involved in such a life-changing experience and consequently it resonated with anyone who had recently given birth.

There were many elements from Mel's real life in the book, whose promo blurb read: *'With her TV career hitting the skids and her daughter's nappy doing the same every two hours, her husband suddenly unemployed and the bank writing to her only in red, Mel needs to come up with a scheme, and fast: move to a house they can't afford, of course! Welcome to an endless cabaret of sleeplessness, removal men, sinister toddler groups, husband-stealing lodgers and competitive mums...'*

But though it dealt with some of the more serious problems Mel was by then facing, it was still very light-hearted. Ben was portrayed as a DIY fanatic, her mother as still being stuck in the fifties regarding childcare, and even the family's lodgers got a mention in the sitcom that was Mel's 'book life'.

It was an easy read, with plenty of laugh-out-loud moments and as an addition to the relatively new 'mumoir' genre, it was firmly in the comedy camp. It was exactly what you would expect from such a talented comic, but some people found it a little far-fetched. 'The situations, though realistic, are played for laughs and as a consequence there is little depth to the characters,' wrote one online reviewer, before giving it 4/5 for readability.

With the book's release came opportunities for publicity, and Mel subsequently appeared to try to reinvent herself as a bit of a celebrity mum. She provided perceptive commentary and articles to newspapers and magazines, talking about things like maternity underwear and the changes women experience after becoming a parent.

The book was successful and popular with new mums. Most reviews were positive and some even mentioned their desire for another sequel. But like most books, it wasn't a bestseller and made a limited amount of money for Mel.

Throughout the rest of 2006, Mel worked sporadically. She narrated the documentary *TV's Greatest Stars* and appeared with Sue as a talking head on *Girls Who Do: Comedy*.

She guested on one episode of the panel show *School's Out*, presented by Danny Wallace, and one episode of *The Best of the Worst*, hosted by Alexander Armstrong, and she appeared on *Countdown* for a week.

But work was getting still harder to find and juggling the relentless job search with looking after two small children must have been incredibly tough, even with Ben by her side. And despite her increasing financial concerns, the year finished on a warm note for Mel. She voiced the popular lead character Mist in the much-loved Christmas TV movie *Mist: The Tale of a Sheepdog Puppy*.

Using real animals and shunning CGI and animation, the story centred around an impossibly cute Border Collie puppy who desperately wanted to become a real sheep-dog.

The other characters were voiced by among others Brian

Blessed, Sandra Dickinson, Derek Jacobi and Una Stubbs, and it was nothing less than an instant classic. It was a real Christmas Day family film, which captured hearts all over the country.

Both Mel and Sue were trying to reposition themselves in the media as solo performers. And both needed to try their hand at a variety of things until they found their new niche.

'I stumble along,' Sue admitted to the *Daily Mirror*. 'But I'd like to continue doing the stand-up alongside radio stuff. And I'm also trying to write a book.'

The arrival of 2007 saw new opportunities open up for both women. The Mist movie had been such a success that it was turned into a series – *Mist: Sheepdog Tales* – which lasted for three seasons from 2007 to 2009. Mel once more voiced the loveable farm pup, joining her former cast members and some new familiar voices, such as Colin McFarlane and Helen Lederer.

She also teamed up with Bill Nighy, Zoe Wanamaker and Damian Lewis to work on *Scene and Heard*, a worthy and unique charitable project that brought together underprivileged young children with actors, playwrights and directors.

The children, encouraged to write their own five-minute plays, got to see their work put on stage by a top cast of acting professionals, while the audience got to snigger at the actors and comedians as they portrayed things like hairy hammers, fleas and dishcloths, and used nonsense lines like 'die, snivellingratcreep-fly!'

'I must be in trouble,' quipped Nighy at one performance in April. 'I identified with the hairy hammer in a major way. As a squid I am taken quite seriously by the under-nines, so I like moving in those circles.'

Mel also guest-starred in an episode of *Holby City* called 'Close Relations', playing a character called Lydia Lazenby, and was a celebrity judge on *Eurovision: Making Your Mind Up*, the show that decided Britain's entry into that year's Eurovision Song Contest.

But perhaps the most exposure she had that year was for Comic Relief, when she took part in *Celebrity Fame Academy* in the two weeks leading up to Red Nose Day. It was a chance for Mel to show off her singing voice to the world – for charity of course. And she was excited but nervous in the run-up the to the show's start.

'My stomach has already started to churn,' she told the *Daily Mail* shortly before it began. 'I've got butterflies and I've been waking up at three, four, five, six in the morning in a cold sweat.'

Competing against her were Roland Rivron, Miranda Hart, Linda Robson, Tim Vine, Zoe Salmon, Angellica Bell, Ray Stubbs, Colin Murray, Fred MacAulay, Shaun Williamson, Tricia Penrose and Tara Palmer-Tomkinson.

They were given training and guidance by Carrie Grant and David Grant, the vocal coaches on the regular *Fame Academy* show, while the judges included Lesley Garrett, Craig Revel-Horwood and academy 'head teacher' Richard Parks. Mel moved into the *Fame Academy* house along with the other contestants and immediately got to work practising.

Colin Murray had his suspicions about Mel and put £50 at 12/1 on her winning the competition. Once the singing began, he felt pretty smug about his choice – hidden underneath those nineties bun pigtails was a surprisingly good voice.

'I knew Mel was really good and I knew no one else knew she was really good,' he said, once the competition had got underway. 'I think everyone thought she was going to be the novelty comedy person and she's surprised everyone.'

Perceptively, Mel was convinced that Tara, who she had instantly warmed to, was the dark horse of the competition. 'She's a trained pianist and could have the voice that makes everyone go "Oh God",' she told the cameras.

TPT would also have another advantage over the other contestants, which she revealed on the first night of the competition. 'I went to boarding school and then another boarding school, followed by finishing school,' she said. 'So I know everything about living with other people.'

It was a fun few weeks. Half way through, the gang went out together to celebrate Radio 1 DJ Colin Murray's thirtieth birthday and were a little worse for wear the following morning – especially *Heartbeat* star Tricia Penrose, who got told off for forgetting her headset.

But she could be forgiven for being distracted that morning, because Mel had decided to pull down Murray's boxers to give everyone a glimpse of his butt. Sue came along to support her comedy pal in the competition, just like Mel who would go to see Sue's stand-up tour when she performed it in London later that year.

Mel did well but was the sixth celebrity to be voted out – meaning she was home and with her family again well before the final. 'It doesn't matter,' she told the cameras. 'Please keep spending your money, keep voting!'

And as Mel had confidently predicted, Tara Palmer-Tomkinson did indeed win the charity competition.

CHAPTER 18

NEW PARTNERSHIPS

'I got sent this mad script and I just thought Christmas had come early...'
Mel Giedroyc, *The Scotsman*

W hile Mel was singing and voicing farmyard animals, Sue was heading into more food-related new territory – this time with journalist and restaurant critic Giles Coren.

As part of a BBC Four series called *The Edwardians – the Birth of Now*, Sue and Giles had been commissioned to present a one-off special called *Edwardian Supersize Me*.

Based around the diet of our Edwardian ancestors, the fascinating programme had the presenting pair dressed in Edwardian outfits sampling the daily menu of the people of the time. It sounds easy, simple, even fun – but in reality it was an epic challenge.

Chef Sophie Grigson was in charge of the 100-year-old menu, which was unlike anything you could imagine. The show explained that the average life expectancy of an Edwardian male was 42, and after watching Sue and Giles live the life of a privileged Edwardian couple for a week, it wasn't difficult to see why: the upper classes quite simply gorged themselves on gargantuan 12-course meals.

It was an eye- and waist-popping documentary, and viewers found themselves fascinated by the duo's seven-day journey through food heaven and hell. For Sue it was particularly hard, as she normally avoided meat in her diet. But both presenters struggled with the lifestyle as well as the diet of the Edwardian era.

Sue was stuck wearing a flouncy dress and corset for the week, which was hard enough without the mountains of rich food that she had to force into her now tightly constricted body.

'With any luck,' said Giles at the beginning of the show, 'the inconvenience of our outfits will be compensated for by an afternoon of stonking home cooking.'

Faced with an overflowing table of dishes on their first morning, both Sue and Giles finally realised what they were up against.

'This is a week's food?' asked Sue.

Grigson just laughed.

'A month's food?'

'Don't be silly,' she replied. 'It's today's food.'

`Sue's slender figure was about to get the same kind of battering she admitted to on *Light Lunch*.

A typical breakfast consisted of porridge, sardines on toast, curried eggs, grilled cutlets, bacon, kedgeree, coffee, hot chocolate, bread butter and honey.

Lunch could be kidneys, rolled ox tongue, mashed potato and macaroni.

Afternoon tea was next – a huge selection of cakes. A standard tea consisted of coconut rocks, fruit cake, Madeira cake, bread, butter and toast and hot potato scones.

The dinner spread was equally stodgy: oyster patties, sirloin steak, braised celery, roast goose, potato scallops and vanilla soufflé.

A lot of the food went to waste – for Edwardians it was more about the spectacle of a huge spread than actually eating it all. There were hardly any vegetables and the diet was mainly protein and carbohydrate based. 'I'm becoming beige too,' Sue announced barely a day into the challenge.

Each day the pair struggled their way through a menu that forced an insane 5,000 calories into their bodies. And by the end of the week they'd put on weight and felt lethargic and unwell.

Sue found it hard to sleep every night because she felt so 'full and dark' and Coren spent a lot of his night-time hours on the toilet. All in all, though, it was a fascinating programme – educational and entertaining, with some very funny moments. Coren's face while contemplating drinking 'raw beef tea' at midnight was chief among them. And viewers enjoyed watching the pair gorge themselves and suffer through the often distasteful menus.

Sue loved working with Giles, and their on-screen chemistry proved a winner with audiences. Fully loved-up, Sue even joked about having a bit of a crush on happily-married Giles and it was interesting to note just how different she was now, acting on screen with men.

She had admitted that since coming out she had found it much easier to be around members of the opposite sex – mainly because the previous weight of expectation was lifted. And she even felt that she could flirt with guys now, safe in the knowledge that absolutely nothing was going to happen.

Well probably not…

'It doesn't mean I don't find men attractive,' she told *Woman & Home* a few years later. 'It does mean that I can flirt outrageously and they think they're safe – they're not! I think men are gorgeous, it's just the balance has tipped for me now. That's why I don't like the label "gay", I believe its fluid. It's not like a club you can sign up to as a kid that you're not allowed to leave.'

It must have been hard for Mel to see Sue so happy with another on-screen partner, and in fact, in hindsight, she has admitted to feeling twinges of sadness during those years. She was proud of Sue, but a little bit of her regretted that she wasn't in Coren's place.

'On a bad day I was maybe wistful and sort of thinking, "Oh why is she doing that with Giles Coren",' Mel admitted to the *Daily Mail* in 2012.

But then she wisely summarised their divergent paths by saying in the same interview: 'You have to be grateful for what you have. I think both Sue and I have things the other would like. I see her life as quite free. She can go in any direction creatively. I suppose she sees the fact that I have children. But we can laugh and talk about it.'

In those years, each woman saw the other as being successful in the one way that they themselves weren't.

As spring turned into summer (and while Sue got her digestive system back on track), Mel received a script from her agent that got her very excited: *Eurobeat – Almost Eurovision*, a comedy musical based on the popular European song contest, set to be performed at that year's Edinburgh Fringe Festival.

Mel had been Eurovision-crazy since her childhood – her family not only watched it religiously every year, but she would perform her own version too, organised by her sister.

She loved the concept of the musical, which had already proved a smash hit in Australia and entailed a comedy staging of the competition, which would have different winners every night, depending on who the audience voted for.

She auditioned for and won the part of Boyka, the flamboyant Bosnian co-presenter of the competition. It was a chance to wear a glittery costume, mad wig and put on a silly accent – and Mel was in her element.

Squabbling alongside her was Sergei – played by a variety of people including Glynn Nicholas, Norman Pace and eventually Les Dennis – Boyka's arch nemesis and former Olympic pole-vaulter. It was exactly the kind of fun work that Mel needed and she threw herself into rehearsals with gusto.

'The first thing the director said to us was, when you go on stage with your flag you must believe you are representing the country,' Mel told *The Scotsman*. 'You don't go on and anticipate the laugh. You are absolutely committed.'

It was now Mel's turn to take the Fringe by storm. Staged at the Pleasance Grand, the musical was a raucous affair right from the first night and people were soon raving about it.

The Scotsman's Andrew Eaton wrote: '*Eurobeat* was the first thing I saw at the Fringe this year and I thought it was an absolute hoot.'

Everyone who experienced it seemed to agree and the audience was packed-out every night, dressed in their chosen country's colours and carrying all the props (like flags and clackers) they would need if they were going to the real Eurovision Song Contest.

Mel was totally committed to the role and gave it her all. And so did the rest of the cast, who played a variety of European characters, including Avla, an hilarious send-up of Sweden's best musical export, ABBA, Italy's Vesuvia Versace, the KG Boyz from Russia, an Icelandic Bjork-eqsue singer, and a Greek Nana Mouskouri lookalike from Greece.

The voting was done by text each night and so the whole cast had to be poised and ready to return to the stage at a moment's notice if their country won at the end.

Backstage was always frantic and sweaty, farcical and exciting. Estonia mostly won, Russia's boyband were never far behind while the UK unsurprisingly (since most of the audience was English and weren't allowed to vote for their own country of course) were generally last.

It was the surprise hit of the 2007 Fringe, and won the Best Musical Production award at the end of the month. Well-respected *Guardian* critic Lyn Gardner reported:

Several of the songs are actually much better than real Eurovision entries and the lyrics are often a clever mix of innocence and innuendo.

Now let's be absolutely clear what we are talking about here: Eurobeat *is to high art what the turkey twizzler is to haute cuisine. It will not be liked by anyone who has ever said: 'I really must go to the theatre', as if theatre is some kind of cultural medicine. There is nothing in the slightest bit improving about* Eurobeat *and like turkey twizzlers it will do you no good at all, but it is darn good fun, and is probably best enjoyed in a large crowd, all prepared to enter into the spirit of the thing.*

It works because it doesn't insult the audience's intelligence and because the production values are high and the cast work their cotton socks off.

No, it's not going to change your life and it is instantly disposable, but only the terminally high-minded would be inclined to award this ludicrously silly and enjoyable show nul points.

It was so successful that it would go on tour intermittently for a year, during which time Mel got to show off her exceptional improv skills.

For instance, when the Icelandic banking collapsed happened in 2008, Iceland's entry in the show – usually very popular with the audience – got booed off stage. Both Mel and that night's Sergei, Les Dennis, walked up to the mic, not quite sure how to diffuse the tension. But Mel had it covered: as the poor Icelandic performer disappeared from view she yelled after her, 'Give us our money back, you greedy bastards!'

'There was a sharp intake of breath and then a relieved howl of laughter from the auditorium. It was as if everyone had been given permission to laugh,' Dennis told *The Guardian*.

Mel garnered particular praise for her portrayal of the pink and shiny Boyka: 'Mel, who has been with it since the start in Edinburgh, has sort of made the character her own, and she's just a joy to work with,' said the musical's co-creator Craig Christie to the website *officiallondontheatre.co.uk*. 'She leads by example, so the company adores her and… the audience also gets an extraordinarily great deal out of the enormous wit and enthusiasm that she brings to the stage.'

But however successful *Eurobeat* was, and however hard Mel was now working, it wasn't enough to save the family's beloved house. In September 2007, with an aching heart, the family put their beautiful Acton home on the market. Frustratingly, it took many months to sell.

'The market was just starting to fall,' she explained to the *Daily Mail* in 2012. 'I thought, "We're going to have to declare ourselves bankrupt if we don't sell this bloody house". I was having sleepless nights. We got through it in the end but it was a tricky time.'

That Christmas must have been a lean affair, and Mel even wrote about it in a roundabout kind of way in the *Daily Express*. She penned a nostalgic piece for the paper about Christmas and the pressures of preparing for the holiday, which that year had forced her to reassess her priorities.

'For me, Christmas was always about presents,' she recalled in the piece. 'As a child, we each had an allotted place in the sitting room for the ceremonial unwrapping and mine was perched beside the telly on a Moroccan pouffe. We would watch our mum with bated breath as she divided up the gifts.

'I remember getting my first portable radio-cassette player – I had prayed for that for months, so desperate was I to have somewhere private to indulge my new-found love of Kajagoogoo.'

Now that she was a parent, she wrote, she finally understood how stressful each Christmas must have been: 'Only now that I'm a mum can I fully understand the terrible pressure parents feel buying presents for their kids. My mum had four children plus all of the extended family and she not only had to feed us all but she bought presents for everyone, too.'

She remembered the years she had previously spent buying pointlessly expensive gifts for people because she had the money but not the time. This year would be different.

'I'm giving all the adults in my family charity gifts – in my case through CAFOD, the Catholic Agency For Overseas Development,' she wrote. 'By giving presents that make a difference, I look like a hero and I'll hopefully make everyone else feel guilty for persisting with their shallow, tat-buying frippery. It's a win-win situation.'

Eventually, after countless stressful months on the market, they sold the house, put most of their belongings into storage, said goodbye to the lodgers and moved their young family into a tiny, rented two-bedroom flat.

'It was this crazy seventies place full of orange velvet and mice, but we had such a laugh,' she recalled to the *Daily Mail*. 'We had no mortgage and none of our stuff, which was really liberating.'

It was a completely new start for the family.

CHAPTER 19

HISTORY AND GLUTTONY

'I think I didn't like food for a while – it was something
I had to eat in order to stay alive.'
Sue Perkins, *DIVA*

Afer its surprise 2007 success, Mel continued to tour with *Eurobeat* for much of 2008, to great critical acclaim.

Her on-stage chemistry with fellow star Les Dennis was lauded by both critics and fans, and when the show stopped in London for a stint at the Novello Theatre she was clearly happy.

Speaking at the show's West End opening night, Dennis even touted the idea of a new double act: 'Mel and I both come from backgrounds of working in a comedy duo [Les worked with Dustin Gee] and we both know that it makes things so much less daunting. We can go on stage and there is no fear, you can just have fun. Working together on something else is definitely something which we've talked about for the future so who knows what will happen?'

Mel seemed enthusiastic too: 'Les came into my dressing room a few weeks ago and said, "We've had Des and Mel, how about Les and Mel?" I laughed at first but the idea's grown on me.'

She was excited to be in the West End with the show, which was a huge sign of its popularity. And although she had no idea what she was going to do if and when the show ended, she seemed calm about her open future.

'I'm a gypsy figure, a vagrant going from one thing to the next,' she said. But while she had mentioned possibly working with Dennis, it was really Sue she wanted to join forces with again.

'We talk about it endlessly,' she said. 'It would be great to do something, but God only knows what…'

Sue was busy with her own new comedy partnership: *Edwardian Supersize Me* had been such a success that the BBC had commissioned her and Coren to do a six-part series in the same vein.

The Supersizers Go… aired in May and featured Perkins and Coren eating their way through six wildly different periods of history. Filming required a huge level of commitment to the project that went far beyond merely reporting factually on the subject.

For each period, the duo dressed in the era's clothes, lived in an appropriate style of accommodation for the period and of course, ate the right diet for the time.

'The immersive element is the thing I enjoyed about it,' Sue told the *Daily Telegraph*. 'One can mass together a lot of facts and statistics about a period, and fire them at an unsuspecting audience, but for this we plunged straight in. We wanted the viewer to get a visceral experience. Whether the food we were eating was making us feel tired, scared, weird, fat, drunk or whatever it is…'

Sue saw *Supersizers* as a history programme, not a food show. Yes there were celebrity chefs doing the cooking but the goal of the show was to educate in an engaging way, and the duo certainly did that. It was a completely fresh way of presenting history, a giant leap away from what was then the current vogue for drama documentaries.

'I think what we tried to do here is look at history through the prism of food, through the prism of sensation,' she told *The Daily Telegraph*. 'What we wanted to do was to go back as much as 600 years and see how other periods speak to the modern consumer.

'I think there are good history programmes around but the ones that resort to spurious dramatisations are not really my bag... I think a lot of television is influenced by a focus group-style sense of what the viewer wants. And the more you have to canvass opinion, the further away you get from delivering something good.'

First up was a WWII menu, exploring rationing with chef Allegra McEvedy. In contrast to the indulgence of the Edwardian era, the duo had to be a lot more thrifty with their food. Sue was in charge of cooking with the meagre rations, which was exactly what she would have been doing as a wartime housewife.

At first it did not go well. Despite the fact that the wartime rationing system had been scientifically designed to keep the population healthy, the duo struggled to use their limited ingredients in a way that would keep them from going hungry.

Vegetables were unrationed and therefore unlimited, but people had to survive on limited items like one egg, two lamb chops, two rashers of bacon, one ounce of cheese and four ounces of special margarine laced with vitamins – per week.

They were vastly unimpressed with the cheap but ingenious vegetable-based 'mock' versions of home-cooked favourites like roast pork and duck, which were enthusiastically endorsed by the era's cheerful Ministry of Food. At one point Sue even resorted to chewing grass – a suggested practice at the time – and it made her mouth turn green.

It was easy to see how the rationing system ruined the nation's palette for years to come, as has often been claimed, but Sue ended up with a lot of respect for the diet.

'It showed you how well you can live,' she told *The Daily Record*. 'Grow something on your windowsill, or get an allotment and not eat too much meat. We ate lots of swede, spuds, carrots and plenty of porridge which is just so good for you. It doesn't sound exciting, but we won a war on that diet.

'Within a week, I felt as strong as an ox, really healthy. Then you go back to eating loads of sugar and you feel shit again.'

Coren and Perkins experienced the Restoration period, the Victorian era, creative Elizabethan cuisine, the Regency period, and the culinary explosion that was the 1970s.

During their Restoration experience, Perkins spent most of the week drunk.

"During that time they didn't have any clean drinking water so you drank small beers from the moment you got up. Even the children drank it," Sue explained to *The Manchester Evening News*. "I was drunk and crying, with laugher I hasten to add, by 8.30pm. One night it got to 9pm and I was slurring and red faced. I passed out and Giles urinated in a bucket in front of four academics dining with us. All of which was captured on camera. I woke up to the sound of him urinating next to my head."

While working on the Victorian era, Sue was in her element. A Victorian woman's diet essentially consisted of sweet treats, according to Sue, which were her favourite things to eat.

'Victorian women just ate cake,' she said in an interview with the *Daily Record*. 'They fainted, took laudanum [an opiate], and ate lots of cake. It was a case of "shut up, my dear, and take the drugs".

'So they'd lie around, take opiates, read a novel, pass out, wake up, have some cake, fall over, pass out again, be put to bed, wake up, have a hysterical fit, have more cake, and then die at 35. It was a lot of fun.'

After filming the Victorian episode, Sue found she had put on a little 'cake weight'. But she didn't mind. 'I ate probably 6,000 calories a day, for ten days,' she said in the same interview. 'But I've never laughed so much. I wore this eighteen-inch corset and had this huge gut full of cake struggling to break through. The cake had nowhere to go. It was lining my heart.'

But during the Elizabethan era dining experience she was left with such a little appetite that she lost it all and then some: 'Basically, the Elizabethans went off to the new world, discovered all these new flavours which they thought were amazing,' she added in the *Daily Record* interview. 'They brought them home, had no idea what to do with them and threw it – all of it – into things they'd already been making. Like fish pie. It makes a late-night Hawaiian pizza really look like a sensible option.

'I lost so much weight it was awful. It almost defies description. Language deserts you when you're faced with eating anchovy tart, with raisins, sweet pastry, dates and cinnamon.'

Despite the yo-yoing nature of her weight and appetite during filming, the programme actually ended up giving her a better relationship with food in general: 'I think I didn't like food for a while,' she explained to *DIVA* magazine. 'It was something I had to eat, in order to stay alive. You know, when you don't feel great about yourself, your relationship with food does go awry. When I don't feel very happy, I just get so skinny. *Supersizers* has given me love handles. It's warped my physique into something I don't recognise. Now, I love food. I love the creativity and expression that goes into it.'

Sue told the magazine that she particularly enjoyed filming the seventies era episode, because she could tuck into the food that she fondly remembered from her childhood. 'It felt like cheating a bit, because I was basically going back to my childhood. I went back to my primary school in Croydon and ate a ton of chocolate sponge and chocolate custard.

'I could see six-year-olds looking at me and thinking "Oh dear, she's a bit of an embarrassment". I ate about half of a tray bake, which was the size of a king-sized duvet. And there was butterscotch Angel Delight after that too. Amazing.'

But although the sweet stuff was as satisfying as she remembered, the savoury was a huge disappointment. 'I remember thinking all that stuff – crispy pancakes and crinkle cut chips – was great. But God, they're disgusting,' she added in the same interview.

Her alliance with Coren was growing stronger and more popular with viewers, despite the pair's huge differences – Perkins was more left-leaning than Coren, he more of a bon viveur in contrast to Sue's 'semi-vegetarianism'.

Their sibling-style ribbing and good-natured rivalry was infectiously funny: Coren was a wimp about some of the challenges they faced during filming, while Perkins had obviously decided just to man-up and get on with it.

During the Elizabethan episode they were presented with a pie full of live frogs and Coren screamed in panic. 'I laughed so much I nearly vomited over the food,' Sue said to *The Telegraph*. 'On the one hand, Giles is incredibly handsome and macho. On the other hand, he's just rubbish. He is a total wuss.'

Sue added that Giles was like a 'male Mel', but was quick to reinforce how much she still cared about her one true best friend. 'Mel is just part of my DNA really. We've known each other 20-odd years.'

Sue was changing and it showed in her work. With every new thing she achieved, every new show she made, she was slowly growing in confidence. And as she approached her fortieth birthday she was learning a lot about herself and how to be happy in herself.

'If I feel confident – and that's not often – it's like I'm flying,' she said to *DIVA* magazine. 'But if I feel I'm working with people who don't think I'm good, if I've had a bad day, or there are lots of shouty people there who just want to take pot-shots and talk over you, then my confidence – which isn't that strong, it's not that big a reserve – gets whittled down quickly. Then I become silent and I can't make jokes. I'll put my hand up – there are so many panel shows where I've got some bad vibe off somebody and just clammed up, because I feel ashamed to be there. You know, usually I'm the only pair of tits in the room.'

For years she had forced herself to appear on a huge variety of TV panel shows, for both the exposure and experience, and had always found it stressful. As a freelancer, Sue never knew where her next paycheck was coming from so she felt the necessity to say yes to most projects she was offered.

But now she was beginning to feel a little more in control of her life and was finding the courage to turn work down. It felt good. 'Of late, I've gone, "You know what? I don't have to do it",' she said in the magazine interview. 'If it's going to make me feel horrible inside, and I'm not going to keep my end up and be a good female presence on that show, then let somebody else do it who's better than me, or who can really stand up to be counted in a slightly more hostile environment. I'm not very competitive. I don't want anyone to feel bad, or be unable to speak or to have their moment.

'All of that's been a very important lesson over the last few years. With it comes an acceptance that there are people who can do certain things a lot better than I can. Maybe that's something to do with being 300 miles away in Cornwall. You can't control everything, so why bother? Actually, it's quite nice to say no, and I can list five people who would be funnier. It's quite a relief to not feel you have to be the best, or pretend to be the best.'

Sue now much preferred to be working in her vegetable garden at home, or taking Pickle and Parker for walks along the stunning Cornish coastline, than fighting her corner on a panel show for a pittance. Who could blame her? Especially since she could afford to be picky – in the previous year she'd earned over £80,000 through her various projects. And in the next project she wisely took on, she absolutely shone.

CHAPTER 20

HIGHBROW MUSIC AND LOWBROW REUNIONS

'If the public wants us back, we'll be back...'
Sue Perkins, *The Daily Record*

B y the time summer 2008 had arrived, both Mel and Sue were happily and gainfully employed. They celebrated Mel's fortieth birthday in June, as well as the airing of a brand new kids' show Mel had filmed over the previous few months, in between *Eurobeat* dates.

Sorry I've Got No Head was a stroke of genius in kids' television programming: based on the recent resurgence in sketch show popularity – *Little Britain* and *The Catherine Tate Show* to name but two – it was a pre-watershed version of the snappy, caricatured adults skits that teens were staying up late to watch anyway.

'Why not give them their own,' someone must have thought, and *Sorry I've Got No Head* was the brilliant result. It had a good cast of grown-up comedy talent – Mel was joined by Marcus Brigstocke, Anna Crilly and James Bachman among others – who brought its unpatronising writing and bold characters to life.

Some of the most memorable included the Fearsome Vikings, who were scared of everything; Britain's most unsuccessful thespians; The Witchfinder General, who called people witches, and got them carted away by peasants; and Ross from the Outer Hebrides, who's school only had one pupil: him.

It was refreshingly well-tailored to its audience and as such was extremely popular. It aired for three series between 2008 and 2011, before spawning another well-received show that Mel would go on to guest-star in – Pixelface, based around what the computer characters from the show's 'Backstage Access' sketches got up to in their spare time.

After the joy of working on the fun sketch show, she returned to *Eurobeat*, before joining forces with Les Dennis on another West End project in the autumn: hosting a one-off performance of *Me and My Girl*.

Mel and Les had been asked to anchor the production, for which the 120-strong cast had only been allowed to rehearse for 48 hours, to raise money for leukaemia charity the Anthony Nolan Trust.

Taking place at the prestigious London Palladium, the performance was supported by Dame Judi Dench, Stephen Fry and Joanna Lumley, and Mel was only too happy to introduce it.

But although many thought it was a sign that the 'Les and Mel' partnership was imminent, once *Eurobeat* finished at the end of the year, their working partnership came to an end too.

Mel was very definitely heading down a more sunny and light-hearted entertainment road, while conversely, Sue's work choices kept getting more and more high-brow. While Mel was filming brilliant and fun sketches for kids, Sue had decided to push herself both intellectually and physically by taking part in a unique new BBC programme called *Maestro*.

At first glance it looked like yet another example of the tired 'celebrity-learns-a-skill' format: a wide range of famous folk competing against each other to conduct the BBC Concert Orchestra at that year's Proms in the Park event.

But in fact it was one of the best pieces of classical music programming the BBC has ever managed, and part of that was down to the skill the participants were learning – the mysterious, and indecipherable to mere mortals, arm-waving of the conductor.

Maestro not only gently explained the intricacies of the beautiful art, but it also showed how absorbing it was to those involved and how important it was to music in general.

For Sue, who had devoted herself to piano as a child, it became nothing short of an obsession. The other contestants included DJ and artist Goldie, actress Jane Asher, presenter Katie Derham, Blur bassist Alex James, comedian Bradley Walsh and actor David Soul.

Each celebrity was mentored over the intense summer-long training by an established, professional conductor and Sue was paired with former assistant conductor of the BBC Philharmonic, Jason Lai.

From the very beginning the competition was taken very seriously by all the contestants, and certain individuals instantly outshone the rest. Jane Asher's intuitive understanding of music (she dated a Beatle for years, after all) was immediately obvious, as was her enjoyment of the experience.

Goldie had a stage presence that almost everyone else lacked and an intensity that made him a commanding conductor, even when he made mistakes. He looked, acted, and believed in the part, and boy did it show. The other clear frontrunner was Sue herself.

Sue had first come into contact with learning music at a very young age. As she admits, she was bookish and awkward as a child and struggled to find a way of expressing the myriad emotions she felt every day. Words and the crafting of them were an obvious outlet. So was music.

But it was a lonely occupation: many exceptional classical musicians find it hard to interact with people because of the limited contact they had with their peers as a child. To excel in music takes dedication and there are only so many hours in a day – socialising is often low on the list of priorities.

'The only problem with music, however, is that in order to get to the point where you're good enough to really feel you're saying something, you've spent over a decade in a room on your own practising scales,' Sue told *The Guardian*.

'I did my grades,' she explained of her musical years. 'I even got as far as an A-level, where I was lucky to be taught by someone who moved me beyond the arpeggios and key changes and mind-boggling mathematics of it all. She made me see how music connects seamlessly to philosophy, politics, history, life. I loved it: it's the only study I've done that I found utterly and compellingly immersive. Then I went and spoiled it all by doing an English degree, and never played the piano again.'

It was something that Sue had obviously regretted for a long time and *Maestro* must have felt like something of a rare second chance. But despite having come to the competition with a modicum of musical knowledge, she felt exactly the same about conducting as all the other contestants: what on earth did they actually do?

'Whenever I went to a concert, all I could see was a middle-aged man with a stiff peak of silver hair waving his arms around in blind opposition to the musicians around him,' she told *The*

Guardian. 'I could not see any correlation between the flamboyant baton-swirling and the music itself. I soon learned.'

Sue threw herself into practising and soon found it to be a physically demanding and emotional occupation.

'These famous pieces of music are in your power for a little while – that's the joy of it,' she tried to explain in the same newspaper interview. 'A great conductor is an alchemical force: someone who can absorb the historical weight of a famous melody, the expectations of an audience and the mercurial brilliance of a host of musicians and shape them all to his or her interpretive ends.'

She wasn't the only one who felt the weight of the task. The contestants' struggles as they slaved away just to make their movements passable were both raw and real, and at one point Katie Derham even stormed out in tears when she couldn't meet her mentor's expectations.

Before the show aired, Sue was at pains to point out how special the show had been as an experience, and how much she hoped people would see it as more than a fly-on-the-wall celebrity competition. 'Whatever the critics make of *Maestro*,' she pleaded in *The Guardian*, 'I hope they don't call it a reality show. Yes, we amateurs are eliminated as the weeks go on; but reality is washing your knickers and slagging off your friend's boyfriend and putting food out for the cat. It isn't standing in a posh suit in front of the finest performers in the world as a sonic boom of beautiful strings smacks you in the chops. That's not reality – not for me anyway. For me, it's pure bloody magic.'

In the finale of the show Sue was declared the winner and no one was surprised.

'I can't believe what I've just seen,' said judge Dominic Seldis after Sue had faced the challenge of Beethoven's 5th Symphony. 'You made conducting Beethoven seem easy.'

What made her even prouder was that not only did the esteemed judges recognise her obvious skill at conducting, but so did the thousands of people watching at home – it was they who voted her into first place. Without them she'd have come second to Goldie, who had completely astonished the judges with his conducting prowess.

She not only conducted at The Proms in front of 30,000 people, but she also proudly led the London Lesbian Gay Symphony Orchestra in recording the score to the cult film *Pervirella* at St Anne's Church in Soho the following year.

It was a phenomenal personal achievement and cemented her place in the public eye as not only a very funny woman, but as an intelligent and cultured television personality.

It would lead to a variety of different work the following year, starting with a lecture she was commissioned to give in January by BBC 2. Entitled *Wit's End? British Comedy at the Crossroads*, it was for the Royal Television Society's Huw Wheldon Lecture and took at a look at the boundaries within comedy as well as celebrating the great British institution. It was an honour to present it and Sue must have felt humbled and excited as she did.

That year, after a few years apart and with the wisdom of age, Sue began to grow reflective about the short-lived *Light Lunch* and her time working with Mel.

'Maybe we could have done a couple more [series] then thought about our careers and planned them, rather than bumbling around like a couple of halfwits without an ambitious gameplan,' she said to journalist Paul English from *The Daily Record*. 'But I think there's still some goodwill towards us, at least we didn't over-stay our welcome. We do still work together. We might try to work up something in the next year or so. We'll do a bit of writing and see how it goes. The will to do something is there and we're very good mates. I think ultimately, we'll see. If the public want us back we'll be back.'

But this time it was no idle comment – it was time for the duo to reunite, even if it was only temporarily. And it would be down to their old pals French and Saunders to make it happen.

In March 2009, French and Saunders, comedy's best-loved sweethearts, were preparing to perform their last sketch together – for Comic Relief.

They had been in the process of retiring from the double act sketch format for a year or so, and were going to finish things off with a real bang for charity. They would still work together on other projects – *Jam and Jerusalem* to name just one – but the sketch show they were so famous for would be no more.

The pair had been best friends for over 30 years and only that year had been rewarded with a Bafta fellowship – the last double act to receive that honour being Morecambe and Wise.

They'd each had successes singly, too – with *The Vicar of Dibley* and *Absolutely Fabulous* – but now they were finding it lonely at the top of the comedy tree. They were still the only truly successful female double act in Britain and that saddened them. Especially since they'd had such high hopes for Mel and Sue.

'I used to think there were quite a few that could have followed us,' French had said to *The Telegraph* two years earlier, at the beginning of the duo's farewell tour. 'I thought Mel and Sue were going to for a while.'

But although popular, their former protégées hadn't worked

together for a good few years now and no one had risen up to replace them.

'I can't believe there aren't at least eight other female double acts on TV by now,' French told the newspaper in the same interview. 'I know telly is a very boysy club, but the boys need girls in comedy – otherwise, it's completely unbalanced.'

Saunders, who was also being interviewed by *The Telegraph*, agreed and put the relative lack of high-profile female comedians at the time down to 'the level of confidence required when you're starting out. Small gigs can be quite gladiatorial, and you need male bravado to get through them. It's a tough atmosphere that not many girls relish. It's easier to be a wacky rude boy than a wacky rude girl. It's more of a fight for a girl in comedy.'

Just a few years later Britain would witness the phenomenal rise of hilarious stand-ups Miranda Hart and Sarah Millican, and of course, Mel and Sue would return. But in 2009 Mel and Sue were still apart and Hart and Millican, although recognisable at the time, were still working their way up the comedy ladder.

For their Comic Relief sketch, French and Saunders needed a huge ensemble cast – because they were planning an epic spoof of the making of the hit musical and film *Mamma Mia!* And they wanted as much of their old gang back together again as possible – including Mel and Sue.

The 'behind the scenes' style musical was broadcast on 13 March, featuring Philip Glenister, Sienna Miller, Miranda Hart, Joanna Lumley, Alan Carr among many others. It was a true swansong – an hilarious spoof of the phenomenally successful stage show and film, which had viewers in stitches.

Mel, in a brunette wig, played the musical's writer and Sue, in blonde, the producer. Side-by-side they appeared on screen for their scene and cheers rang out in living rooms across the country.

'I think the genius I had was to think of ABBA,' said a serious looking Sue, fully in character.

'Yes, yes,' agreed sidekick Mel in a ditzy voice. 'And I really had to put the words in between the songs. And remember a story I'd heard about a slut that sleeps with three men and gets preggers and the kid wants to know who her dad is. Back of fag packet stuff.'

'Made us very rich,' nodded Sue. 'And friends rang us up and said "You've got to make a movie of this!" So we did!'

They had exactly the same chemistry, were completely at ease with each other and it was as though they'd never been apart. It made the both of them yearn to fully reunite their partnership. They just needed the right project…

CHAPTER 21

CHANGE IS COMING

'I always thought that if I didn't get a job because of the way I looked, it probably wasn't a job I wanted. I'm not a sex object, nor would I ever want to be.'
Sue Perkins, *The Daily Mail*

After temporarily reuniting with Mel for the brief comedy respite that was Comic Relief, Sue moved straight on to filming another series of *Supersizers*, which was still very much in demand.

Supersizers Eat was the next and final incarnation of the show, and featured Coren and Perkins immersing themselves in the eras of Ancient Rome, Medieval England, The French Revolution, and the 1920s, 1950s and 1980s.

It was fun but tiring filming the time-travelling foodie series. For the Ancient Rome segment Sue dressed in a toga and longhaired wig and raced around Parliament Square in the manner of the warrior queen Boudicca. The famous female leader's usual horse was replaced by a much more manageable jeep.

At first, onlookers gawped at the scene, but eagle-eyed tourists and passers-by soon noticed Sue's trademark glasses glinting in the spring sunshine.

'I look like Al Murray in a Cher wig,' she said during a break in filming. 'Or Cher after she's spent the night in a Biffa bag. I'm worried I'm going to be arrested.'

Coren, meanwhile, was busy strutting around in full-on Emperor attire, pretending he wasn't enjoying the dressing up. Producer Alannah Richardson told one journalist from *The Scotsman*: 'It's comical because he comes to wardrobe and pretends he doesn't like putting the outfits on. He starts off obviously acting and then he really gets into it. He denies it every day of course.'

Sue had found this series fascinating to film from a feminist point of view. 'It's quite incredible," she also told *The Scotsman*. As a whole, women have been on a bloke's arm for thousands of years – which I'm not very good at anyway. We've travelled from 100BC to the 1980s and the only job I've had is a part-time one at the travel agents. There's always been a lot of cleaning, but I very nearly went mental this series during the 1950s. Cleaning was all I did. You can make a few jokes about it, then it just becomes boring and claustrophobic. I know what it's like to be liberated – and to go from that to the sound of a clock ticking for a decade was really hard.'

During the fifties episode, Sue dressed in a pinnie and stayed at home cleaning while Coren went off to work. As he skipped off in the morning, she yelled at him: 'Enjoy your liberty! Your freedom!'

The presenting couple's weight yo-yoed again, a fact confirmed by the regular weigh-ins both had as part of the show. Half way through the series, she revealed: 'At my last doctor's weigh-in, he said, "You are 28 per cent body fat". My brain immediately translated that to, "You are one-third butter and you simply can't eat for a week".'

But it was hard to maintain consistent health when eating was her job – especially when filming the French Revolution episode. 'I ate things that almost made me cry with joy,' she said in the *Scotsman* interview. 'We did a whole meal just about cakes. There were huge sugar towers, Viennese biscuits and the finest communion wafers. In the corset I wore, Ros Little, the head of costume, managed to lace my waist down to 22 inches. But the thing is, all of the fat squeezed out of the top of my chest and became Jordan-like. I had these huge hooters! The second I took the corset off, all of it dropped to my gut, like a spacehopper of fat, leaving me with pancake-flat boobs again. Perhaps I should be thinking about doing a diet DVD.'

The pair celebrated the Coronation of Queen Elizabeth II, indulged in an 'orgy', drank champagne with pop tarts and played at being Lord and Lady of the Manor.

They ate 5,000 calorie-breakfasts from the 19th century and then survived on vitamins and laxatives in the twenties to explore the very first diet fads. 'We've got the mix absolutely right,' said the show's producer. 'It's history meets food meets comedy; there are three quite strong themes. So the relationship between Coren and Perkins is really important. They play off each other really well. They are both very different: Perkins is the right-on comedienne; Coren plays the public school Oxbridge boy. If they were both the same, it could fall a little bit flat.'

Coren finally admitted that Sue was a lot braver than him when it came to her pallet. 'Sue will always go that extra mile when it comes to eating,' he said to *The Scotsman*. 'I think it must be something to do with women having a higher pain threshold.

Or the fact that because she's veggie, she doesn't realise what she's letting herself in for. I think there's a mentality of, "If it's a steak, it might as well be a fish eye". I will draw the line, but she will keep going. In fact, she's just eaten some cow's udder pate. Even our hardened cameraman, Big Chris, was dry-heaving at that.'

It was another successful *Supersizers* series, but also the last. 'Sue and I can't just keep sitting at tables, pulling faces and making smart remarks about the food,' Coren added in the interview.

It also must have been a relief to stop feeling so ill all the time too: Coren regularly suffered from headaches, diahorrea and vomiting during filming, while Sue's digestive system often went into full-on rebellion at processing such different foods to what it was used to.

When the series aired in the summer, Perkins was highly praised for her presenting skills, leading one reviewer to ask: 'Why isn't Sue Perkins more famous?'

'Watching the current, fabulous *Supersizers Eat* series a vital contemporary telly conundrum struck me,' wrote *The Guardian*'s Jane Graham. 'What to do with Britain's best and least famous TV presenter? If talent, intellect and sparkle had anything to do with it, Sue Perkins would be the most highly paid female TV presenter in Britain.'

It was an interesting point. Sue had everything going for her, so why did she still have such a relatively low profile?

In *Supersizers*, Coren was the main presenter, really – introducing Perkins as his sidekick at the beginning of each episode. But it was Sue who garnered the most laughs and as many agreed, regularly outshone him.

'She is modest where he is maniacal, usually funnier than him and exhibits a depth of knowledge about history and the arts almost equal to that which Coren imagines he possesses,' wrote Graham.

It was true: although they had a dedicated food researcher on the show, Sue would gladly spend hours reading about the different periods and foods they were experiencing, just so that she could truly understand what she was doing and make educated comments and quips in front of the cameras.

And during the 2009 series Perkins proved more than a match for not only Coren but also the various guests they invited to join them for dinner on the show.

'In the last few weeks we have seen her match Diana Quick for charisma, Michael Portillo for worldly sophistication, and Toby Young for zeitgeisty bon mots (too easy, I know),' Graham summarised.

'What does it say about British telly that this 39-year-old woman – intellectual, sharper than most of her male counterparts, undemanding and fair-minded – seems doomed to a much lower profile?'

The same question could easily be asked of Mel, a witty, talented and erudite author, actress, presenter and comedian – who at that point was earning just £200 a week treading the boards in a low-budget London play.

Mel was starring opposite the young *Skins* actor Nicholas Hoult in *New Boy*, a coming-of-age play put on at The Trafalgar Studios that spring. Based on a William Sutcliffe story, Mel played a teacher who has an affair with one of her students – the new boy in school – consequently 'taking' him from the sexually confused friend who has a crush on him.

Her exceptional performance was much appreciated by the critics. Lyn Gardner enthused: 'Mel Giedroyc is toe-curlingly funny as the French teacher who once gave a detention to a boy who was staring at her breasts, citing "excessive attention to irrelevant detail", but who is transformed into a self-deluding fool when she falls in love.' Another critic said that she 'pleases with another amiably psychotic turn'.

But the play itself fell flatter than a pancake with the critics lining up to take acerbic pot-shots: 'The plot turns into a load of ropey old nonsense'; 'The writing is uneven and the storyline pretty preposterous'; and 'It's a shame the play doesn't take you anywhere or say anything of worth. The actors deserve more'.

Mel definitely deserved more – she had too much experience and talent to be earning such a small amount and going so far under the radar, even if she was acting on stage, which she loved.

Back in Cornwall that summer, Sue was hard at work on her next project: as one of the judges of that year's Man Booker Prize for Literature. It was a tall order, which involved reading a book a day, but it did mean she could stay at home and spend some quality time with Kate and the dogs.

For the time being, life was still good in the idyllic eighteenth-century cottage. In between reading the Booker entries she regularly made the short drive to the coast to pick up fresh fish for tea and tend to her lovingly cultivated vegetable patch.

The year before, they'd harvested broad beans, runner beans, beetroot, potatoes and courgettes. Coming from Croydon, Sue had no real history of green fingers – but she had taken to growing things like the proverbial duck to water.

At weekends, the couple would have a leisurely breakfast, often outside, before taking their dogs down to the nearest beach for a walk. Pickle and Parker – being inquisitive beagles – would often run off, meaning hours of searching for the mischievous pair. Then everyone would go home for lunch and the dogs would cuddle up to sleep next to the family cat, Moss, a lovely old thing.

As well as her vegetable garden, Sue also had a greenhouse, where she often spent her Saturday afternoons. She fed the tomato plants, examined the chillies... and updated the comedy diary she kept about her garden exploits.

Sue was already in the middle of writing a book – one of the many she had started and abandoned over the years – and everything was a writing opportunity for the literary buff. But like many intelligent literature lovers, she hadn't the confidence in her own work to get it to the point of publication. The fear of not being good enough was always there – too much to bear.

The cottage was quietly busy with art and literature and nature and friends. It was a life filled with watching owls at dusk, cosy pub lunches on Sundays, baking cakes at the weekend, endless cups of tea and long evenings watching box sets.

As Sue approached her fortieth birthday that September it appeared that things were pretty perfect. Yes, she still wanted children but she was thinking about fostering. She had a long-term girlfriend, dogs she adored, and though she wasn't top of the British celebrity tree, her skill and wit was now in regular demand.

Cornwall had been a great leveller: being surrounded by farmers and fishermen she was in constant contact with people who were living in harmony with the earth around them. 'I've learnt to be a much more exterior person with a lot less in my head,' she told one journalist.

But although it had been such a positive influence on her, sadly, Sue wouldn't live her picture-perfect cottage life for very much longer: the next few years would bring seismic changes in both her personal life and her career.

Sue spent the rest of the year working just outside of Sheffield. After her success on *Maestro*, Sue had been approached to undertake an unusual job – revive the fortunes of South Yorkshire's Dinnington Colliery Band.

She jumped at the chance to work on a music-oriented programme again – she'd been looking for something exactly like it ever since she'd won the conductors' reality show the year before.

But even if she'd been hesitant, the footage she was shown of the two matriarchs of the band, sisters Kay Brookes and Joan Herman, would have convinced her. As she told the *Telegraph*'s Naomi West: 'They made me roar with laughter. There was Kay saying, "We were ont' march and one of the band fell down a manhole and we carried on walking because we didn't want to miss a beat". I thought, why wouldn't you want to spend a few months being around them?'

Sue pretty much relocated to Dinnington for the rest of the year. The town was far removed from her Cornish coastal world, but exactly what she had expected: 'A faded little high street with Poundstretcher shops, charity shops, a mobility scooter shop…'

The colliery had been closed since 1992 and the band hut, 'which looked like some sort of public lavatory', was right next to the bus station. Sue felt very conscious, going into her first rehearsal, that she would be more of an annoyance than anything else. She knew nothing about life in that part of the country or the struggles of the miners and their families, but Sue's natural warmth and the community's embracing collective nature got her instantly accepted.

'I just blustered in and we connected very quickly,' she said in the same interview with *The Telegraph*. 'I formed a witches' coven with Sally and Penny [Kay's daughters]; there was a lot of banter way too rude to be shown on television.'

What constituted the band was unlike anything she had expected: Sue had conducted orchestras, been to the Proms, loved classical music all her life – so she had no idea what to do with the 'piecemeal and squeaky' sound the six band members made at Sue's first hearing.

She immediately knew what to do first and cheerily set about trying to recruit more players, her enthusiasm only slightly dampened by Kay and Joan's resigned and negative attitude.

'They'd tried everything to get people interested in the band, and it hadn't worked. But I felt that you wouldn't get people to come if there is an atmosphere of depression in the band. There are kids playing "Guitar Hero" at home: why would you do that when you can make a real sound in a real space – and make some friends?'

Slowly the band began to grow and slowly – with the help of brass band guru Dr Nicholas Childs, director of the famous Black Dyke Band – they began to improve. It was an honest and uplifting show, its striking realism made even more powerful by the very genuine words and actions of the group. No one played up to the cameras, it was as if they weren't there. No one faked enthusiasm or happiness.

When Sue excitedly told the group that they would be performing at the Rugby International between England and Australia, then was a tumbleweed-style pause before Kay announced: 'Oh, I don't like rugby.'

Sue found the whole experience very emotional, and was moved when the band asked her to be their honorary president. 'It was not on camera, which makes it all the more sweet,' she said.

While Sue was working hard filming with the band that autumn, she was in no way absent from British television screens. Firstly she appeared in yet another food related show, the brand new Channel 4 quiz *The Big Food Fight*. The basic premise was that each week, gastronomic guru Hugh Fearnley-Whittingstall would be challenged by a different chef guest captain to see who knew the most about food.

Each culinary team captain had an obligatory array of celebrity guests on their team to help/hinder them in answering quick-fire questions and blind-tasting certain items, showcasing their knowledge on everything from cooking to shopping and growing to eating.

Sue's pal Giles Coren appeared on the fourth episode, an experience he was keen to write about in *The Times*: 'I did a TV game show this week with Sophie Dahl. Some others, too, but they're neither here nor there. All you need to know is that there was me and a supermodel, alone under lights, quite heavily made up in front of a large audience, raring to answer the quizmaster's questions. Well, quizmistress. Okay, it was Sue Perkins. Obviously. I am not allowed on telly unless Perky Perks is there to hold my hand and keep me calm, and make sure I don't punch anyone or try to light my farts.'

Apart from Coren and Dahl, guests included Levi Roots, Heston Blumenthal, their friend from *Supersizers*, Allegra McEvedy, and Greg Wallace. It was funny and different, with a generous seasoning of surprising food facts.

Barely a month later she was back on TV presenting a

programme called *The Art on Your Wall*, showing the influence that her artist girlfriend Kate was having on her. It was another cultural offering, this time taking a look at the changing tastes in domestic art in post-war Britain. It examined the mass-market masterpieces and pictures in people's homes and was an interesting insight into how wall space has been decorated over the decades.

After a jam-packed few months, at Christmas that year Sue returned from Sheffield, and she and Mel received a surprising new offer.

CHAPTER 22

REUNITED FOR
A BAKE OFF

*'It's just people in a windswept tent making scones. I think the
Olympics cemented our idea of what it is to be British and part of that is
to endure terrible weather conditions, the village fête and judging cakes.
Then you have Paul Hollywood who looks very earnest with his piercing
blue eyes, and Mary Berry who's the nation's sweetheart and brings
a real class to it. A class that Mel Giedroyc and I do our utmost to
undermine with our really weak jokes.'*
Sue Perkins, *The Sunday Mirror*

When Mel and Sue were first approached about presenting *The Great British Bake Off* they had very different reactions to the job offer. Sue initially said no because she didn't think it was anything particularly special. She was in the process of marking out her TV territory in a more intellectual vein and a show about sweet and edible things didn't fit in with that at all. Also, she didn't think it would last more than one season.

'They said, "Would you do it?" and I said, "No, it's about cakes, don't be silly",' she explained to Jonathan Ross on his show in early 2014. Conversely, Mel was keen to take the gig because she was still struggling financially. She had managed to avoid bankruptcy, but was still trying to dig herself out of her money problems and the job would bring in a good wad of much-needed cash. But like Sue, she didn't think the show would last.

'When Sue and I said yes to presenting it, in my heart of hearts I thought: "This is just another cookery show – there are plenty of those already",' she later told the *Metro*. 'I thought it would go under the radar but I needed the work and it was a chance to work with Sue again. We hadn't worked together on TV for a while, so I thought it would be a laugh.'

In the end they both agreed to take on the presenting role and filming began on the first series in April 2010. Every weekend they travelled to a different location around the country, on the hunt for Britain's next star baker.

Working alongside cake queen Mary Berry and professional baker Paul Hollywood, both women settled back into their presenting partnership very quickly. They were at ease in front of the cameras and brought a warmth to the show that cut through any of the tension from it being a competition.

'On the first series I was worried because we hadn't worked together for a while and we were older,' Mel told one *Daily Mail* journalist in 2012. But to anyone watching they were the same loveable gaffe-prone best friends they always had been. They messed around a lot with the props, cracked terrible jokes and tried not to eat too much cake – something they both failed miserably at, since they each put on nearly a stone during filming.

'I've put on a good 11lbs every series,' Mel revealed to the *Radio Times* in 2012. 'The first couple of episodes it's, "No thank you, not for me". Cut to the semi-final and we're hoofing up whole quiches.'

Since filming only took place on spring weekends, it didn't affect their day-to-day lives very much at all. Sue even had time to start filming another unrelated programme during the weekdays. But they both enjoyed being back together on the show, interviewing the contestants, revealing interesting tidbits of baking history and presenting the whole competition.

After just over two months, filming finished and Mel and Sue went their separate ways again. *The Great British Bake Off* would air in August and both of them believed that would be the end of it – that the programme would sink into oblivion faster than a dodgy soufflé.

'None of us knew what we were doing,' Mel later admitted to *The Daily Mail*. 'I thought, "We'll probably be slagged off really badly if anyone watches it, but I don't think they will". I remember phoning Sue and saying, "Right, don't panic. There are 5,000 cookery shows on television. No one's going to give a monkey's about a bakery show. But we've got a bit of cash – move on to the next thing".'

And move on they did. Mel went back to acting, and appeared in an episode of the popular comedy *Miranda* as a life coach. She also filmed another series of *Sorry I've Got No Head*, the kids sketch show that was being so well received by target audience and critics alike.

Sue scampered back to TV hubby Giles Coren, this time to continue filming *Giles and Sue Live the Good Life*, the programme she'd been working on at the same time as *The Great British Bake Off*.

As with all her projects with Coren, Sue fully immersed herself in the experience, moving to a suburban street in North London with Giles for the show's three-month-long filming schedule.

Based on the popular seventies sitcom starring Felicity Kendal and Richard Briers, Giles and Sue had decided to recycle the fictional format into a reality TV show, in which they would live entirely self sufficiently for the summer. They grew their own vegetables, used a methane generator to power their electricity and even wove their own material for clothes.

And at first they were about as adept at it as Tom and Barbara Good had been: on the first day Coren tweeted, 'I actually touched a live chicken. Terrifying. Could have ended up 2010's Steve Irwin.'

With typically acerbic wit, Sue replied: 'When you say "you touched a chicken", it makes it sound active. Actually, a chicken inadvertently grazed past you and then you screamed.'

The duo could get advice from experts if needed, but most of the time they were on their own, finding solutions to problems as diverse as carrot blight or constipation in pigs. Though Sue had a bit of experience with gardening, thanks to her Cornwall homestead, Giles was a complete novice. And he was terrified of animals.

'They can suddenly turn and bite you and poo on you and they're unpredictable,' he told a fellow journalist in a *Daily Mail* article with deadly seriousness. 'And they make sudden "Raarg" noises, like children...'

In his role as a food critic, Giles was clearly much more used to eating animals than rearing them, but dressed in dubious seventies outfits, he and Sue painstakingly converted their new little back garden into a farm and brought in a small coterie of animals: Pinky and Perky the pigs, a cockerel called Lenin, and goats called Geraldine, Jet and Laura.

Using a 1970s rotovator, just like in the sitcom, they planted strawberries, cucumbers, courgettes, garlic and cabbage, before erecting a chicken coop and painting it a very fetching hot pink.

Soon after, 12 hens were delivered and the couple had fresh eggs every day until the chickens got anal mites.

Sue had to hold them upside down while Giles filled them to the brim with mite powder. 'That was a low point,' she confessed.

And although having goats meant they had fresh milk every day – eight pints of the stuff in fact – it did mean that they had to be milked daily. Luckily Sue proved to be a natural.

The summer went quickly and had its highs and its lows. At the end of the self-sufficiency experiment, both Perkins and Coren agreed that being entirely self-sufficient was a full-time job – 'but you can take bits of it,' said Sue.

She found the time to muse on the changes that had taken place in society since *The Good Life* was on TV in an article for *Homes & Antiques* magazine, in which she'd recently started penning a monthly column:

Much has changed in our attitudes towards food and the environment. When the show first went on air in 1975, it was the ludicrous attempts of Tom and Barbara to leave the rat race that provided the amusement, whereas in the 21st century it seems more natural to scoff at their neighbours – the scandalously wasteful and crass Margo and Jerry Leadbetter.

We no longer aspire to drink gin and tonics on a Day-Glo sun lounger whilst phoning Harrods for a jar of ox tongue in aspic. These days, the middle classes long for a patch of land to call their own on which to milk goats and pull reassuringly bent and muddy carrots from the earth.

Coren was surprisingly sentimental about their summer of self-sufficiency. 'The truth is, the good life is a wonderful but almost impossible dream,' he wrote for *The Mirror*. 'If I had a bit of land in the country I could have a crack at it. But I haven't. And I never will have. But to do it in a small suburban garden is probably crazy. I was inspired by the show to plant tomatoes and artichokes and courgettes in my back yard at home, and they came up okay. In future, when I have children, I might get some chickens. I might grow some vegetables, build a few things from scratch, but I won't run a small dairy farm, or power my house with faeces. Sue and I had the most fantastic summer, and I think we made a fun television show. Now it's time to get back to reality.'

But for Sue, there wasn't much time for reality – because life immediately got a whole lot more unbelievable for her, when *The Great British Bake Off* aired on BBC2 in August.

In the beginning, no one quite knew what to make of the programme – was it '*Masterchef* done by the WI', as *The People* newspaper decided, or 'just another cookery show', as Mel and Sue had both initially thought? The one thing that critics were in total agreement on, however, was that it was great to see Mel and Sue back together again. In fact, it was all anyone could talk about.

'Mel and Sue were once as inseparable as the layer of jam in a Victoria sponge and the lower slice of cake,' wrote the *Liverpool Echo*, upon announcing the show's first episode:

You couldn't get them apart without a lot of scraping and it would leave an awful lot of mess and crumbs all over the place.

    Gone are the days when the double act were a reliable mainstay of telly, standing for the sort of non-threatening, gently amusing chuckles we all count on to get us through the bleak and lonely hours. Mel had gone off to have kids and Sue had thrown her lot in with Giles Coren, taking the galloping gourmand time-travelling in The Supersizers.

Or so we thought. Now they're back, reunited to test the mettle of Britain's amateur bakers – all vying to be crowned the number one bun-maker in the country. Yum.

The *Birmingham Mail* celebrated their return as well, while at the same time lamenting that *Light Lunch* was still not being resurrected:

They were once the bastions of daytime telly, a duo you could rely on for great gags and good food – and then as a partnership, they disappeared from view, seemingly gone forever...

Well, fear not – Mel Giedroyc and Sue Perkins are back. But sadly, they haven't decided to revive Channel 4's much-missed Late/Light Lunch *format, though rest assured they'll be offering up something just as tasty in* The Great British Bake Off.

Considering the struggles the pair had gone through since *Late Lunch* had finished, it must have felt nice to have so much support from the media – even if it did mean their cookery show was never going to go under the radar, like Mel had predicted. Typical was this comment in the *Daily Telegraph*:

This sweet and floury six-part series, like a more homely version of MasterChef, *is based around a contest between 10 of the UK's best amateur bakers. That means button-pushing back stories, nervous looks through oven doors, trembly hands applying icing and apron-clad displays of emotion. Indeed, there's so much blubbing here, it's a wonder the confections don't all taste too salty.*

Hosts are Mel Giedroyc and Sue Perkins – a duo who boast a baking background, if you can count their Nineties ads for Kingsmill bread. This fondly remembered comedy double act worked with French and Saunders and went on to front cult daytime show Light Lunch. *They've since gone their separate ways: Giedroyc into acting and motherhood, Perkins to numerous panel games and talent shows. So it's a treat to see them reunited, although there's not nearly enough of their witty repartee here…*

A treat indeed: Mel and Sue fans hoped it wasn't a one-off, and they were rewarded with a TV phenomenon that would keep the pair on their screen for years to come.

In that first season of the show, the comedy duo were clearly feeling their way through their new presenting roles. Everyone had their place – Paul, Mary, Sue and Mel – and they would find them soon enough.

Mel explained to *The Daily Mail*: 'By the second series we thought, "Oh hang on. Our role's a bit more like this: we're the cheeky bookends and Paul and Mary are the meat of the show".'

As the first series progressed, more and more viewers tuned in. It was well-paced and surprisingly gripping and captured something beautifully indefinable.

Sue said to *The Daily Telegraph*: 'It's in keeping with our make-do-and-mend recession culture and it's about spending quality time with people. There's also a wonderful slowness to the programme; you can't hurry the baking of bread. Then there's Mary Berry – who reminds everyone of their mum or their grandmother – and there is Paul Hollywood, who is sort of tough but fair. There is also the baking itself, which at times reaches sublime levels.'

It certainly was a good combination. And maybe its success was a matter of good timing too: the Women's Institute had recently reported a 60 per cent rise in applications for its baking courses, and baking demonstrations had been selling out up and down the country before *Bake Off* had even begun, and afterwards the country would go a little bit crazy for cakes.

Whatever that magic ingredient was, the nation was soon hooked on *The Great British Bake Off.* By the time Edd Kimber was announced as the show's first winner in September, Britain had salivated over sticky marmalade tea loaves, gone teary-eyed over brownie meringue cakes with raspberry cream, and wondered, awestruck, how to recreate maple and pecan bread – it was food porn and it was addictive.

It had amassed viewing figures of up to 3 million and quickly jumped to No 1 in the TV station's ratings. No one could believe it, least of all Mel and Sue, who were nothing short of amazed by its popularity.

They were quickly commissioned to do another series the following year and Mel in particular heaved a huge sigh of relief at the news. '*Bake Off* did come about at a really good time,' she said in 2013. It had literally saved her career – putting her back on the celebrity map and generating important new work offers. And it helped to get back on her feet financially too, and she and Ben soon managed to buy a modest new home in Ealing with a small garden. It was nothing like the house they had overstretched themselves for before, but it was home, and Mel would never again take financial security for granted.

In late autumn, riding high on baking success, Mel joined the touring cast of *The Vagina Monologues*. A global phenomenon, the revealing show was a perennial touring sensation, with over 4,000 shows having been performed worldwide since 1999. Mel was understandably nervous – the monologues were very intimate – but it was a fun tour, with some memorable moments: in Southport they even had a very unusual guest on stage, as Mel described to the *Glasgow Evening Times* when she later arrived in the Scottish city to perform the show.

'It was a great crowd,' she recalled in the interview. 'Then we were joined on stage by a male streaker. None of us could speak for 20 minutes. 'He was dragged off stage and chucked out a back door into freezing Southport butt naked. I have to say it was truly a proud moment.'

Whilst in Glasgow for the *Vagina Monologues*, Mel was also encouraged by comedy legend and friend Andy Gray to visit the Oran Mor theatre and take in its popular lunchtime series, *A Play, A Pie and A Pint*. The experience moved her deeply.

'It was buzzing; full of actors and writers and it is that kind of central place where everyone comes together,' she raved in her interview with the *Glasgow Evening Times*. 'You just don't get that in London – there isn't that sense of community that you have. I loved the idea of exchange of ideas over a drink and a different play every week. It felt like a very creative hub. I was completely bowled over by the place.'

Mel was inspired and knew she wanted to get involved somehow. But straight after *Vagina Monologues* it was time to head back to

London to start the second series of *Bake Off*, so whatever she was planning would have to wait.

While Mel's home life was now settled – and both women's careers were definitely on the up – Sue's personal life was sadly becoming turbulent again.

Her relationship with Kate was beginning to fall apart and Sue was starting to feel like she was losing control of things again. She'd just turned 40 and marking it had kicked-up a whole new world of feelings and fears. It would soon be time for another monumental change for the comic.

CHAPTER 23

TASTING FAME AGAIN

'It's busy, busy and long may it continue, it's all good. Life is sweet.'
Sue Perkins, *The Northampton Chronicle*

The year 2011 was a hectic one for both Mel and Sue. After being 'almost famous' for over 15 years, now they had finally hit the big time. They were TV prime-time fixtures, overnight successes after decades of hard work. *The Great British Bake Off* was popular all over the world and the two presenters were being recognised everywhere they went.

It was exactly what they had always wanted. The only problem now was fitting in all the work they were being offered: not only were their schedules rammed with new work but every magazine and newspaper wanted time with the pair too. Mel and Sue were happy they were back together, and now they had the best of both worlds: a comedy partnership and successful solo careers.

Apart from *The Great British Bake Off*, Mel filmed another series of *Sorry I've Got No Head*, starred in new kids TV series *Sadie J* and acted in a boiled-down version of the classic Shakespeare play *A Midsummer Night's Dream*.

Sue was just as busy as Mel. In March she picked up the conductor's baton again, for Comic Relief. But this time the musicians weren't trained, they only had one instrument and they numbered in the thousands. But this was no Philharmonic Orchestra – it comprised a mixture of celebs and the general public wielding plastic kazoos.

Staged at the Royal Albert Hall, Sue guided the 3,997 musicians through playing 'The Dambusters', creating a new world record in the process: for the largest kazoo ensemble.

Next, she 'married' Giles Coren – to celebrate the impending Royal nuptials between Prince William and Kate Middleton. In the BBC documentary *Giles and Sue's Royal Wedding*, the duo examined various royal unions over the years to discover the motivations behind them.

They revealed that George VI married Caroline of Brunswick because otherwise Parliament wouldn't clear his debts; Henry VIII married Anne of Cleves to cement his new church with a European alliance; and Victoria married-off her countless children to various European royals in order to take over the whole continent. Well, sort of…

And after planning an exhausting royal bash, the duo duly sat down to a lavish historical wedding banquet, *Supersizers*-style. Corset straining already, Sue then rejoined Mel for *The Great British Bake Off* in the spring.

The second series of *Bake Off* was filmed slightly differently to the first: instead of travelling round the country, the whole thing was filmed in a marquee in the grounds of Valentines

Mansion, a seventeenth-century mansion house in Redbridge, north-east London. It meant less travelling for the presenters, which was a relief.

Both Mel and Sue were a lot livelier this season, having clearly settled further into their presenting roles. Sue even appointed herself 'chief taster to the bakers,' who weren't always happy about her lingering presence. She carried a spoon around in her pocket to try any ingredient she could see and left nothing unsampled.

'One person had a bowl full of cherries and I ate half of them,' Sue told the *Bradford Telegraph and Argus* in an interview. 'A shout went up of, "Where are my cherries?" and I 'fessed up. Of course they needed all of them, and there were no more cherries in the building. Their end tart was really spartan, so I had to say, "Don't judge it badly – because it was my fault!"'

As during the previous year, the duo had a lot of fun filming the kitsch cookery programme. 'I'll be doing a take and suddenly this huge plastic cob will get walloped against my bottom and I'll just leap into the air,' said Sue in the same interview. 'Or we'll look up fart noises on the iPhone which we'll pop into each other's pockets unsuspectingly, so you'll be doing a link and suddenly this horrible farting sound will come from your trousers. It's a playpen!'

And they had the bakers in stitches with their witty remarks, which were a great way of defusing any nervous tension. During one scene, Sue picked up a jug of liquid and said: "Ooh, is there alcohol in that? Goodbye..." before grabbing the jug and walking off.

Introducing one episode, Mel said: 'Bakers are fighting for their lives... Is that too dramatic? It's never too dramatic. It's cakes, biscuits and desserts we're talking about...' Sue then added: 'Plus I let a tiger loose in there.'

And, of course, there was also the obligatory innuendo – *'Keep an eye on your jugs!'* (Mel) *'Get those ladyfingers soggy!'* (Sue)

But all joking aside, the baking competition was surprisingly heated for being centred around something the country saw as such a gentle pastime. Tears flowed each week as cakes didn't rise, or bottoms revealed themselves to be soggy, and as the final approached, Mel and Sue found it harder and harder to engage the contestants in the cheery banter they'd enjoyed at the beginning.

'At the start of the series, there's a convivial atmosphere and a sense of: heigh-ho, we're all in it together,' Mel said in an interview with the pair for the *Radio Times* later that year. 'But once we're at the semi-final stage...'

Sue interjected: 'They hate us. We try to talk to them, to make a gentle joke: nothing. You could be Michael Jackson resurrected, moon-walking on top of a pain au chocolat and they wouldn't care.'

But it was at that point in the proceedings that their roles changed from cheeky lively presenters to much-needed shoulders to cry on. The duo soon figured out that they were also there to console and support the contestants in moments of crisis.

'If people are in a panic then Mel and Sue will help them,' Mary Berry told the *Daily Mail*. 'The atmosphere is lovely. I wouldn't have taken part if I had been expected to make nasty comments. The combative style of most TV competitions puts me right off. I don't see any reason to shout or swear or be hyped-up. I want to encourage the contestants to bake, and people at home to think that they can make it too. It's not just entertainment, it's a giant cookery lesson.'

But while it was true that the show was a lot more genteel than the usual calibre of cookery programmes – which were usually resplendent with screaming celeb chefs – it didn't mean there weren't moments of drama.

'The competition is insanely intense,' said one of that year's finalists, Holly Bell, in *The Daily Mail*. 'We're all being very British and saying we just want everyone to do well. But inside we're saying, "Die, one of you, die!"'

And although Paul Hollywood and Mary Berry were kind and fair, they were also demanding judges. Mel once said of Mary: 'She's absolutely wonderful, and a total inspiration but does have a core of steel…'

As well as sampling the contestant's creations, both presenters were getting more and more into baking themselves – so much so that Mel and her sister were even getting competitive about it too: at a family party that year, when Mel was outshone by her sister's apple cake, she was more than a little miffed.

Once filming was over on Series 2, there was no time to rest: Mel immediately sped up to Glasgow to appear in a Shakespeare play for her pal Andy Gray – at the Oran Mor theatre. It was only the second time Mel had ever done Shakespeare: the first was when she was at Cambridge and was cast in an experimental production of *King Lear*. She'd played Edgar while the four men and four women all took it in turns to play the Fool.

'All of us had shaved heads and urine-coloured pyjamas with ribcages sewn on the front,' she recalled to *The Independent*. 'It was a radical cross-gender production. We took it on a beige-coloured coach around Europe. My brother said it was the worst thing he'd ever seen. God knows why I was cast. I was always up the back of the stage with a friend, just crying with laughter. I hope students are still pulling that kind of stunt.'

This time she was playing Titania the fairy queen for the *A Play A Pie and A Pint* series she had been so impressed with the year before. Various newspapers questioned why she would travel 400 miles to appear in a low-budget production for peanuts when she was now in such high demand. She had numerous answers, including that she'd do anything for her friend Andy.

'I just said to Andy, "If you're involved, I'm there"', she told *The Glasgow Evening Times*. 'My adage is always say yes. Even with the slightly odd things because you never know. The strangest things can open mad doors.'

But maybe it was the fact that she could now do anything she wanted, and she was going to do whatever made her happy: including writing her very own play.

During a whisky-fuelled conversation that summer with Oran Mor's producer, actor and writer David McLennan, she agreed to write her own play for the series. He gave her a deadline: March 2012.

When the second season of *Bake Off* began to air at the end of the summer, the public had the same reaction as they had the year before – millions of people tuned in and were gripped by the dainty baking show.

Like Mel and Sue, they were also being inspired to get back into the kitchen and soon the show was being held responsible for a 1950s-style return to baking in pinnies and kitsch outfits – ironically the very thing Sue had so hated and rebelled against on *Supersizers* while filming the 'Fifties' episode.

But in whatever way, baking was becoming hip again and the new trend sent the demand for baking products soaring: Marks & Spencer reported sales increases of up to 20 per cent in ingredients, while John Lewis saw a 46 per cent rise in sales of three-tier cake stands and cake tins and muffin trays. Kitchenware specialist Lakeland sold 3,500,000 disposable piping bags just in the first half of 2012, and homeware retailer Dunelm Mill also saw a surge in sales of cake tins and cooking utensils. As its chief executive Nick Wharton happily told one newspaper, 'Baking is becoming ingrained in the British psyche again.'

The stereotype of the middle-aged domestic goddess was being overhauled as younger and younger people were asking for kitchenware for birthdays and Christmas presents.

According to a survey carried out by Leisure Range Cookers that autumn, teenagers and those in their early twenties were responding to programmes like *Bake Off* much more than the older generations. In fact, they were now six times more likely to bake something from scratch every day compared with any other age group.

In a press release, Leisure Range Cookers commented: 'On the surface it may seem like a surprising development that baking is enjoying such a revival amongst the younger generation, but there are a number of key trends that support these findings.

'The younger generation has grown up watching a host of TV chefs; they are on first-name terms with the likes of Sophie Dahl, Lorraine Pascal and Nigella. In fact, a third of people take their inspiration from TV cookery shows. Then there is the popularity of shows like *The Great British Bake Off*, which has been a clear ratings winner.

'Homemade can also mean more economical, and we often see consumers going back to basics during a recession. In tough times we also return to the more traditional practices of our parents and grandparents. All these factors combined have fuelled a generation of food lovers, interested in doing it for themselves as part of their everyday life.'

Big retail businesses like John Lewis and Lakeland were obviously reaping the rewards of the nation's new baking obsession, but craft bakeries and cottage industries were also seeing real growth too. The number of independent bakeries in the UK was (and still is) growing – between 2011 and 2012 there was a 5 per cent rise – and self start-ups were becoming even more prolific. New baking ventures increased by 325 per cent between 2009 and 2013, according to a report by insurance brokers Simply Business.

'These ventures are pumping money back into the British economy,' retail advisor Bill Brown told the *Daily Mail* in 2013. 'They're giving communities jobs. Baking may not yet be up there with manufacturing in terms of value, but it's faster in terms of growth. It's accessible: you don't need lots of expensive equipment and it's something you can do from home with minimal overheads and little or no staff costs.

'The mark-up is good, too, with a gross profit of 70 per cent quite normal. Indeed, cupcakes sell for an average of £2 each yet cost just 20p to 30p in ingredients.'

The humble cake was becoming a hero of our times, as journalist Ruth Tierney commented in a *Daily Mail* article: 'We're baking them, buying them, selling them, reading and watching TV programmes about them. While the global economy crumbles, an army of bakers has been beavering away in kitchens throughout the land, selling scones and cupcakes and, more importantly, acting as a powerful rising agent for national revenue…'

Mel and Sue were at the centre of a fascinating phenomenon and once more everyone involved with *The Great British Bake Off* was astonished at the effect the show was having on viewers:

a record 5 million saw grandmother Joanne Wheatley crowned 'Queen of *The Bake Off* that autumn.

They also saw something else quite astonishing on the finale: a squirrel proudly displaying his nuts to the nation. 'All eyes should have been on the delicious array of cakes and pastries prepared by the finalists of the *Great British Bake Off,*' reported the *Daily Mail* the day after the final. 'But winner Joanne Wheatley's moment of glory had to play second fiddle to a squirrel.'

A camera shot, surveying the general beauty of the filming location, had lingered for a little too long on the very masculine rodent, causing a tidal wave of comments to flood the Internet. One viewer joked: 'This evening's *Great British Bake Off* contains full-frontal squirrel nudity which some viewers may find startling.'

Another announced on twitter during the show: 'A squirrel is flashing everyone on the *Great British Bake Off.*'

Others were admittedly a little more disturbed by the image, saying that it was unnecessary and an unwelcome distraction. Since the programme was recorded months before, it could easily have been edited out. One viewer commented: 'Why did the cameraman focus on the squirrel at all? I just didn't need to see that.' But most found it yet another funny quirk to their favourite show and the shots of the squirrel soon went viral.

Both Mel and Sue were bowled over by the show's overall popularity, and yet more requests for interviews came flooding in. 'I couldn't believe that anyone would notice or really take to yet another food show in the way that they have. There's something about baking,' Mel told the *Radio Times*. 'It's all those childhood memories: family, school fairs, your failed home economics class,' added Sue.

Mel agreed: 'And it's about people's desire to slow down: to get off the rollercoaster of modern society. You can't hurry a loaf of bread. You have to wait for it to prove and rise.'

Sue quipped in response: 'It's awfully hard to make bread on a rollercoaster.'

CHAPTER 24

HEARTACHE AND THERAPIES

*'Writing is important to me exactly because I was trapped
in my own head as a child. It's something I've always wanted to do
and something I'd ideally like to make the mainstay of my life in
the future. You can't prat about forever.'*
Sue Perkins, *The Scotsman*

While in public Sue was joking around and clearly enjoying
the growing success of *The Great British Bake Off*, privately
she was struggling to adapt to the changes that were taking place
in her personal life. She had relocated from her beloved and idyllic
homestead in Cornwall back to North London with her beagles,
and her relationship with Kate was finally over, although things
were still amicable between them.

It was a defining time for the TV star, perhaps even more so
than when she had struggled with revealing her sexuality to the
public, over a decade before. She was just coming to terms with
having turned 40, and she now found herself alone and renting
again. The whole experience felt very seismic and her life now felt
very transitory.

Mel was married with two beautiful children, as were most people
Sue's age. She had wanted that kind of conventional family life too,

225

but it was becoming more and more apparent that motherhood would probably not be an option for her. That realisation, along with her loneliness and solitude, deeply saddened her: she must have felt as if she was right back at square one in her life, and she sought therapy to help her explore her feelings.

'I found turning 40 very difficult – it made me think about things I'd never really thought of before,' she told *Woman & Home* a few years later. 'Like the fact I'll never have natural children. Not having a family of my own at that time felt very painful, and it made me think that one day I might like to foster or adopt, or at the very least mentor young people. It was a tough time, but you do get these little stumbles, and whenever I do, I'm very good at putting things in perspective.'

Slowly, she began to see that as difficult as it was for her, it was also very freeing: Kate had been adamant that whatever Sue did next she must continue writing and now for the first time, she felt like something had been unlocked inside her.

'I spent a lot of my thirties wastefully locked into thinking I wasn't good enough,' she told *Reader's Digest* retrospectively. 'It was easier to say other people's words or to improvise, because if it went wrong you could say, "Well, I did it on the spur of the moment".'

But something was changing inside her, and she suddenly felt a little more able to push past her confidence issues. 'In my forties, I found my confidence,' *Woman and Home* reported her as saying. 'I think I just got to the point where I was so exhausted with my battles of low self-esteem that I just gave up and thought, I have two choices: I can either carry on with this cloak of self-loathing, or I can shrug it off and see what happens. So I did the latter, and it was such a liberating thing.'

Partly, it was to do with undergoing therapy, which she was not afraid to admit to having. 'Well, if you'd lost sensation down your left side, you'd see a doctor,' she told the *Daily Telegraph*. 'So when you're desensitised through depression, or events in your life have been extremely painful, why shouldn't you have some therapy?'

It was clearly working for her. 'I think it makes you a better person and it affects your relationships with your family, your friends, your interpersonal and sexual relationships, too,' she said, adding: 'My view is, "Go on, treat yourself and everyone who loves you to being a better and clearer person". There is shit that I just don't want to carry around forever and so you park it and that's good. I'd tell anyone who is sad or confused to do it.'

But another reason for the emotional breakthrough that was coming her way stemmed from an experience she had that autumn – when she took part in the Sky Arts show, *First Love*.

Sue didn't really think much about what it would entail when she agreed to do the programme – rather rashly, she later admitted. But it would take her on an emotionally reflective journey that, in her fragile state, would break her apart completely before building her back up again.

Sue was tasked with relearning the piano, something that she had abandoned as a teenager after years of intense study. The show charted her journey through the experience, which included six weeks of expert tuition and would ultimately end with Sue performing at a classical concert.

The process began by taking her back to her old school and the exact piano she had reached Grade 8 standard on. 'Oh God it's the same fucking piano!' she said, before walking straight back out of the hall. Finally sitting down at the piano unlocked so many emotions and fears that she found it 'more terrifying than anything that had gone before'.

As a child, Sue had found music to be a much-needed form of self-expression: at first it had helped her, as a shy child, to come out of her shell. But it wasn't long before her overriding fear of not being good enough then paralysed her exceptional playing ability completely.

Sitting down and playing at school assemblies was more terrifying than anything she had experienced in her short life, but even so, she had once been proud to do it. 'I hadn't had a happy relationship with the piano,' she told *The Daily Mail*. 'I'd actually stopped playing when a new girl had come to the school and been asked to play in assembly, like I used to do. She was so much better than I was. I couldn't deal with it. I was such a perfectionist then that I never wanted to do anything unless I could excel at it. And I felt I couldn't excel at the piano. So I gave up. And ever since, the thought of playing filled me with self-loathing.'

Watching the new girl play Chopin's Fantaisie Impromptu so perfectly had ensured that Sue would never again feel good enough: she wouldn't take any risks in case they resulted in failure, she wouldn't push herself past her safety zone in case she accidentally revealed what she perceived to be her ineptitude – in case she revealed herself to be the fraud she feared she was.

Years later, moving her fingers gently over those same piano keys again literally unlocked all her inner neuroses – her brittle perfectionism, her abject fear of failure, her inability to express emotions as effectively as she desired and her bittersweet memories of childhood, all spilled out on what turned out to be a painfully honest programme.

'I'm the sort of person who mumbles, "I love you",' she confessed to *The Daily Mail*. 'I find emotions difficult and embarrassing. The trouble is, music is all about emotions, and to do it well, you have to let all that out.'

Though viewers would by now be used to celebrities 'opening up' on these sorts of shows, with Sue it felt more visceral. She was newly single, a little bit broken, confused about herself and her life and now she was publicly taking a very painful kind of journey into her childhood – the camera just happened to be there. And to make it worse, she couldn't hide behind a shield of humour, as she so often had before in her life.

'That's why it was so terrifying,' she concluded in the same *Daily Mail* interview when filming was over. 'I've gone through my whole life relying on humour when things are difficult. Here, I couldn't. And it taught me a lot about myself.'

When Sue finally stepped out on stage to play piano at the Cheltenham Festival that year, in front of hundreds of classical music fans, she was not only facing a childhood fear, she was facing the one thing that had held her back all her life – the idea that she just wasn't and never would be good enough.

But from the very first note, she was nothing short of spectacular. It must therefore have felt so calming to finally take that risk she'd always avoided – the risk of trying and failing – and succeed instead.

She played Beethoven's Pathetique, a highly emotive, unravelling sonata, and many of the audience were moved to tears. Jazz musician Neil Cowley – who had helped her through her intense weeks of learning – was jubilant. 'I think we all fell in love with you,' he told her after the clapping had stopped.

Sue learnt a great deal about her issues through the experience, which was something she genuinely hadn't expected. This, combined with her continued therapy, gave her a new sense of clarity. Slowly she began to emerge from the fog of suffering she had been trapped in.

'Once you've come through the shock and depression, you think, hang on a minute, I don't want to waste any more time with my head down feeling ashamed,' she told journalist Daphne Lockyear from *Reader's Digest* a few months later. 'Of what? I'm going to stop wasting time and start writing. And I'm very glad that I did.'

She finally began to write with a sense of purpose, just as Kate had hoped with her parting words. What began to emerge was a work of fiction whose roots lay in her own life experiences. And through writing she began to analyse herself and her life so far.

'I've always thrown myself into love in a rather carefree way, and the net result is that you do get hurt,' she told *The Daily Telegraph*. 'But I wouldn't take away any of the experiences of my life,' she admitted. 'When I was younger I used to leap from one relationship to another and I hadn't been single since the age of 16. Basically, I always thought I was better as part of a unit.'

Now very much a single woman, she wanted to prove that she could be a whole person without a partner. A partner needed to complement, not complete. Proof of her new confidence came in the form of showing her writing work to others, something she'd always been terrified of doing.

Sue had actually been toying with her story idea for years previously, an idea that involved a 'benign kidnap' or intervention. 'I knew that I wanted to write about someone who was stuck and whose friends decided to take drastic action to save her from her own inertia,' she explained to the *Radio*

Times a year later. 'I did nothing about this idea. Why? Well, it was so much easier to earn a living doing pieces to camera in stately homes. (Most of my television career has involved opining while walking along lavish corridors...)

'But something strange happened. Slowly the idea took shape. I didn't will it into being; it just metamorphosed behind my back – out of view. When I actively came to look at it again, the story had evolved a little. It had become the narrative of a woman who couldn't deal with telling her parents she was gay. On her birthday her exasperated mates bundle her into a car, and, with the help of a security guard, drive her north to her parents' house so she can come out to them. It was both a literal and existential journey, I told myself – in a vain attempt to appear clever.'

Sue became fixated on the idea, and plucked up the courage to speak to her agent, Debi Allen, about it. Allen loved the idea and pushed Sue to take it further. The next thing she knew she was sitting in a bland BBC meeting room speaking to an enthusiastic comedy commissioner who explained they wanted to take the idea further.

Leaving the meeting, Sue actually couldn't believe she'd even got that far with her little story. She'd always expected to be called out on her mediocrity, not encouraged and supported. The BBC had suggested that the idea be evolved into a six-part comedy drama, and for that her initial idea had to change somewhat. Sue had a lot of work to do – because a first episode was immediately commissioned.

She quickly learned how to formulate plots and storylines and wrote the pilot just in time for an all-important table-read, which took place just before Christmas.

A handful of TV execs sat with a very nervous Sue as a group of actors read through her script. It was an awkward experience, especially since the canny comic would be able to tell instantly what everyone thought of her work.

But laughter rang out in the room and Sue was both surprised and relieved to hear it. 'I clung on to that,' she later said.

She would have to wait months before she heard whether the show would be commissioned, which involved an anxious wait. But she was now confident that, slowly, she was picking up the pieces of her broken life and forging a new path for herself – one that would push her further and lead her to the kind of achievement she'd always wanted.

Sue and Kate's split had been revealed to the public by the *Daily Mail* in January 2012. 'I've just come out of the biggest relationship of my life, so I'm taking it easy at the moment and being a bit gentle with myself and yeah, that's sort of it,' the *Mail* quoted her as saying. She didn't want to explain any more. She was gathering herself back together again but she was still fragile and needed some time to herself.

In that same month, Mel also picked up her pen again – not to write a book this time, but a play called *Slice*. She too had overcome a similar fear of failure to Sue in order to write it, except that her boost had not come through a painful break up, but when Oran Mor's David MacLennan had given her a strong drink and a deadline. 'It's something I'd really wanted to do for years and years but was too lazy or scared, or a combination of the two, to embark on,' she said.

While Sue was inspired by her recent emotional breakthrough – and her life so far – Mel was inspired by *The Great British Bake Off*, the show that had made her so happy over the past two years.

For both women, writing was a fine way to spend the cold and usually depressing post-Christmas months.

'I found the process totally absorbing and addictive, once I'd got over the whole fear factor of actually writing a full-length piece,' Mel told *SG Fringe* magazine. 'I've written tons of sketches and the odd half-hour thing, but never something like this before. I just had to plunge in, I suppose. The weather was absolutely rubbish after Christmas, my kids had tonsillitis and I just holed-up at home and bashed out a first draft between dispensing antibiotics and Calpol. I absolutely loved doing it.'

Somehow the two best friends had both finally found the courage to do what they'd always wanted to, and now both their worlds were truly opening up.

Slice was performed at Oran Mor in March, with a light and fluffy Victoria sponge cake baked during each performance. As Lauren Paxman wrote in *The Stage*:

Great British Bake Off *presenter Mel Giedroyc's debut is, perhaps unsurprisingly, a kitchen sink drama all about cake.*

Three very different sisters are all brought together by the imminent death of their mother. But it immediately becomes clear why it is decades since they last met.

While diligent-to-the-point-of-irritation Victoria furiously beats away at a cake mixture, her older sister Madeleine bursts into the kitchen full of arrogance and innuendo. Little sister Charlotte is the spark that lights the fuse between the siblings, though, with her smug talk of idyllic family life.

Over the course of the comedy, each sister has her turn at being both the craziest and the unexpected voice of reason, with great performances from Lesley Hart, Louise Ludgate and Fletcher Mathers.

The absent, and much-detested, mother is represented by a voiceover – used to great dramatic effect by director John Bett – giving a series of strict cooking instructions on how to avoid making a 'craggy' sponge.

Giedroyc is unlikely to win any playwright awards quite yet, her characters come a little too close to being caricatures. However this is a competent and mouth-watering first effort that whets the appetite for more.

It was a fine writing debut, which was so well received at Oran Mor that it was given a slot at the Edinburgh Fringe a few months later in August.

CHAPTER 25

BAKING BAFTAS AND COOL LESBIANS

'That's what I love about life. It's the weird curve balls.
The soggy bottoms too.'
Mel Giedroyc, *The Daily Mail*

Alongside their intense writing endeavours, 2012 was an exceptionally busy year for Mel and Sue. And their efforts weren't fruitless in the slightest: in January the duo discovered that *The Great British Bake Off* had been nominated for a prestigious Bafta award.

Though they would have to wait until May for the results, it was an incredible achievement just to be nominated and showed just how popular they and the baking show had become in just two years.

In February, Mel went back on the road for a week with *The Vagina Monologues*, alongside Anne Charleston (Madge in *Neighbours*) and Hayley Tamaddon (Delilah Dingle in *Emmerdale*). She clearly loved doing the show, as she kept returning to it – she'd even done another week-long stint before Christmas, just a few months previously.

'I've been doing the production on and off for a few years now and it's a lovely show to dip in to,' she told the *Hull Daily Mail* that month. 'The cast is always changing and you get to do different monologues, which keeps it fresh. Every person who takes part brings something different to the table each time.

'I enjoy the range of material it includes,' she added. 'There's slapstick, wordy parts and such clever stuff thrown in there, along with a couple of pretty harrowing monologues. It also touches on the topic of rape, which is really serious. For me, I love doing the funny parts. It's always good to go back to doing live comedy. You get a good response.'

A week was the perfect amount of time away from home, and she was clearly in a good place in both her home and work life. Flossie was now 9 and Vita 8, and juggling her now successful career with motherhood was obviously a challenge, but one she was rising to in style. 'Life at home is chaos,' she told *The Western Daily News*. 'Ben and I try to share the care of our children 50-50.'

Sue was also busy. In April, she travelled to Laos to film an episode of *World's Most Dangerous Roads*. She'd already filmed one in Alaska with Charley Boorman the year before – an epic adventure that saw them wrapped up tight and tackling the infamous Dalton Highway in an icy ordeal.

Now she was on the Ho Chi Minh trail with Liza Tarbuck, a route through the Vietnam jungle that had been set out by the Viet Cong, mainly to supply their southern attacks on US troops during the sixties.

It was a dangerous trip. She had described her time in Alaska as a 'near death experience', but this was another level: she and Tarbuck were the first women to drive the trail alone – they met machete-carrying tribes who had never seen a Western woman or a car, and travelled with the knowledge that at any moment, if they veered off the trail, they could be blown up. 'Those mountains are littered with unexploded bombs dropped during the war,' Sue told the *Metro*.

It was a hard and emotional shoot and she barely slept. She also didn't have much in the way of phone reception, so when her phone suddenly rang, deep in the jungle, she was surprised to say the least. But she was even more shocked when the voice at the other end of the line told her that her TV series *Heading Out* had finally been commissioned.

It was really going to happen: she was really going to write and star in her own TV show. She cried with happiness.

Back home, the duo started filming the third series of *The Great British Bake Off* and Sue worked on writing the remaining episodes of her comedy drama. Both Mel and Sue knew exactly what they were doing on the show now and this series would definitely be the best yet. An incredible 7,000 budding bakers applied for the show that year, and whittling them down to the final 12 must have been nothing short of a military operation.

But once they were chosen, Mel and Sue met them at Harptree Court, in Somerset, where Series 3 was to be filmed. It was an unusual series, because the three finalists were all male, showing yet another change in baking trends. At first it had been the women who were putting on their pinnies in some kind of 1950s renaissance and whipping up delicate creamy icing in the *Bake Off* kitchen. Now it was the turn of the men, who injected a more modern and technical feel to the show.

As usual, the presenting duo tucked into a wide variety of treats and cajoled and supported the contestants as they tried their best to impress judges Paul and Mary.

It was fun and inspiring and they couldn't believe that something so enjoyable could be considered work.

'It's a difficult show to do,' Sue said in mock seriousness on the Jonathan Ross show a few months later. 'Because we work for up to ten minutes every three days.'

The audience roared with laughter.

'I'm a husk [at the end of filming] let me tell you. I sort of pitch up and say the word "Bake!" in a slightly sarcastic way – I might vary the tone a little bit – then I go off. If something happens people will run towards you wearing those earpieces Madonna wears, yelling "cake is down, cake is down!" And you'll run back with them and there will be a splattered tart tatin on the floor, and tears, and then you do a sad face... I can't tell you how joyous it is. I am the luckiest person alive.'

They both felt especially lucky to be working with such great colleagues. 'We both adore Mary,' Sue enthused to *The Sun*. 'She is just the most humble, sweet, fun-loving and charming person. She is just like a little kid but is also like your grandma.'

'Mary represents the really good side of Britain,' added Mel. 'While Paul is like having a pesky, teasing older brother around the place. He's always there to have a poke and a prod at. We are a bit like a dysfunctional family. I'm the annoying older sister.'

'And I'm the fat one!' Sue said, punctuating the interview. Sue wasn't and never had been fat. But she had certainly experienced yo-yoing weight throughout her TV career and this time she had decided to accept the situation.

'I put on nearly two stone each series – and I mean two stone,' confessed Sue. 'And I know I'm going to do it. There's a pigeon belly. After that, it's a no-cake diet for six months.'

While Sue had obviously decided not to hold back during

filming – who could with all that temptation around – Mel was still battling with ways to try and combat the weight-gain, or at least to limit it. 'I thought for the start of this series I would wear a really, really tight pair of skinny jeans,' she told the tabloid. 'It's a good way of knowing whether the boat is being pushed out and I have to pull back.'

In May, right in the middle of filming, *Bake Off* won its first BAFTA. Mel and Sue joined Mary and Paul and the *Bake Off* team at the glitzy black-tie ceremony, where they celebrated in style.

'Who would have thought that baking would become such must-see TV?' asked host Kate Thornton, in an interview with the cast and crew.

'Not us,' replied Sue, making everyone chuckle. 'That's why we've got this look of complete shock on our faces.'

'If you'd told me I'd get a Bafta for *The Great British Bake Off* I would literally have laughed in your face,' said Mel. 'Sue and I took that gig thinking, here we go, another cooking show among thousands of cookery shows. We enjoyed making it, nice people, loved the bakers, blah, blah... But, oh my God, it's been amazing. It's ridiculous that we get paid to do it because Sue and I just have a laugh and eat loads of delicious cakes.'

May was also the month that *Tatler* proclaimed Sue to be one of the country's coolest lesbians. The high-society magazine had compiled a list of prominent British lesbians in order to raise awareness of gay women, and Sue was pretty much top of their list.

It was a big step forward for *Tatler*, whose pages were usually filled with well-born ladies and refined upper-class clothes and pursuits. Now it was 'coming out' in style, with an edgy ball and an issue dedicated to the country's best-known lesbians.

'In comparison to gay men, gay women are virtually invisible in society so it's about time we did something like this,' said editor Kate Reardon in *The Times*. 'In English society there is a kind of weirdness about lesbians – people either seem frightened of them or titillated by them. There's a huge double standard. Gay men are entirely accepted in society and gay women aren't. Lesbianism is only all right if it's a joke and you're doing it to turn on your boyfriend. The attitudes are Victorian.'

It had been a long time since *Tatler*'s Conde Nast stable-mate *Vanity Fair* had bravely featured K D Lang on its front cover, being shaved by Cindy Crawford – 19 years in fact.

'That was a huge step forward that everyone remembers but it was a long time ago and none of us have done anything substantial since,' Reardon said in *The Times* interview. 'I'm not a moron, I do know this will get attention, but it's not gratuitous,' she said. 'If anybody is shocked and upset by this then they are shocked and upset by homosexuality.

She added: 'We are nailing our colours to the mast and saying, as of now, gay women are wonderful. And if there's some sweet girl at boarding school who is reading this issue and has been too embarrassed to come out to her parents because nobody they know is gay, then actually we can make a step towards normalising it. With any luck, the impact there will be from this is that gay women inch a little closer to parity with straight women and gay men.'

It was a huge step for Sue too, especially since she had been asked to be one of only four women to be profiled in its special August issue. In contrast to a decade ago, Sue was now comfortable with her sexuality and attended the *Tatler* Lesbian Ball that month dressed in a stylish black suit from Paul and Joe. Invitations to the event had read 'No boys allowed' and guests included others on the list like actress Sophie Ward, model Eden Clark and Sue's ex, Emma Kennedy.

Maybe her relaxed attitude had something to do with how the perception of gay women had changed in the years since she came out. 'Lesbians are diverse,' wrote Dr Layla McCay in The Huffington Post. 'They have long hair and short hair and medium-length hair; they wear dresses, jeans, high heels, flat shoes and medium-height shoes; they are friendly, rude, clever, less clever and everything else that makes up any population. Their looks don't dictate their personality. They aren't some sort of other; they're neighbors, teachers, doctors, artists, bus drivers and ballet dancers... and they're as normal a part of society as anyone else.'

The event was a glamorous affair and Sue looked happy to attend. She was in the middle of writing her very own TV series, *Bake Off* had just won a BAFTA and now she was being celebrated in a high-class magazine. Despite a rocky 2011, life was beginning to taste sweet again.

In late August, the third series of *Bake Off* began to air and the country was once more caught in the throes of a sugary addiction. It leapt to BBC 2's number one slot immediately, where it remained for the duration of the series. Nearly 4,000,000 viewers tuned in to watch the first episode, while nearly 7,000,000 gripped fans were watching by the time John Whaite beat Brendan Lynch and James Morton to become Britain's top baker 2012.

Once more, during the weeks that it was on TV, British newspapers were filled with how Berry and co were making baking cool again, and journalists trying to cleverly sum up the show's appeal for their readers.

Mary Berry, just after receiving a CBE that autumn for her lifelong services to the country, gave it a try herself: 'It's a different programme,' she said to *The Guardian*. 'It's not a teaching programme, but people learn from it. Viewers can watch the contestants doing challenges and see how people like themselves – amateurs – cope. Then they think: "I could have a go at that". It's very fair. Many cookery programmes are so hyped up; this one isn't. The aim is not to make people unhappy, or cry. It's all very peaceful and we want them to do well, and if they're doing it incorrectly then we can have a chat to them, perhaps at the end, after they've finished filming, and say: "If you do it like this..."'

But there was absolutely no doubt that part of its success was the light-hearted friendliness of Mel and Sue, who many believed had been destined to present the show ever since their *Light Lunch* days.

Sue in particular felt that a media career that had so heavily involved food had led her and Mel to be the perfect duo for the popular show. As Mel told one journalist: 'The bakers need the humour as well, in this strange environment with cameras on them, being asked to describe everything they do.'

And the contestants needed their gentle encouragement and good-natured sympathy too. 'They're far too modest to admit it,' wrote *The Sun*, 'but one of the key ingredients in making *The Great British Bake Off* so appealing has been Mel and Sue themselves.'

The Independent's Ben Laurence described the duo as 'the icing on the cake' and the unsung heroes of the show, and devoted a whole article to them. 'Mel and Sue are important for a number of reasons,' he wrote. 'Firstly, their chemistry is terrific. The pair has known each other since Cambridge and they have an easy familiarity on screen which never feels forced. Their friendship chimes perfectly with the cosiness of the show and as they totter around the baking tent they put you in mind of two chatty middle-class ladies let loose at an up-market village fete.

'Secondly, they are very good at putting the contestants at their ease. They speak to the stressed-out bakers not with the uninspiring frivolity of a Holly Willoughby or a Tess Daly, but with genuine interest and concern. Perkins in particular is good at rather sweetly comforting distressed contestants, although some may feel like wielding their rolling pins when she clumsily tries to help them avoid a culinary disaster.

'Finally, they are funny. They are particularly adept at bringing Mary Berry and Paul Hollywood down from their judging thrones with a perfectly timed quip. The humour can have a gently surreal edge – "Victoria Sponge backwards is 'egnops airotciv' which is actually Latvian for Mary Berry" – or it can be littered with engagingly bad puns. But it's always good clean fun, impeccably delivered.

'Mel and Sue may not be able to tell a pithivier from a patissier, but without them *The Great British Bake Off* would be a much duller place.'

CHAPTER 26

HEADING OUT

'Being gay is about the 47th most interesting thing in my life, and I think that's the case for a lot of gay people. It's not this big, defining thing that people assume it must be. It's quite ordinary, really. It's not about incessant sex or camping it up in Rio. It's the guy working in the call centre and going home to pay his bills. It's the woman behind the counter in Boots.'
Sue Perkins, *The Daily Mail*

While the country was going bonkers over bagels on *Bake Off*, Sue was still hard at work on *Heading Out*. She had worked tirelessly on penning the project and described parts of the experience of writing it as 'brain-achingly hard'. But buoyed along by her friends and family, and by the faith that everyone including the BBC commissioners had in her, the first draft was finally written by the beginning of the autumn.

She then found herself on the next step of the journey – sat in a freezing cold church for rehearsals and fine-tuning.

'For the first time, I heard the lines in the mouths of those they were meant for,' she later told the *Radio Times*. 'I was so awe-struck by the cast, I completely forgot that I was actually in the show and that I too was required to give a performance. A few weeks later, I was in a make-up chair starting the most enjoyable five weeks of my working life.'

Filming was a blast. She had drafted in the absolute best people for the job – her best friends. Mel obviously had a role, as did Steve Pemberton, Dawn French and her old housemate Nicola Walker. 'I made *Heading Out* with a lot of love and surrounded myself with brilliant people who challenged me to do my best, and also gave a great deal of love and support back. As a result, the experience was blissful,' she told the *Sunday Mirror*.

Ever the professional, Dawn had politely asked Sue to send her a script with a covering letter for her to consider. 'If Dawn had agreed to do it as a favour for a friend then I'd have thought, "Do you really like this?"' Sue told the *Sunday Mirror*.

And she also got a whole host of other actors and actresses whom she greatly admired to take part too, like June Brown, Mark Heap and the stunning Shelley Conn.

'I set out with a wish list of who I'd love to have playing certain characters, never thinking they'd say yes, ever. And then they all did. It almost makes me tearful thinking about that, as it's such a big thing for people to get behind your first project.

In one of my first scenes with Mark Heap, all I could think was, "That's Mark Heap!" You can see on my face I'm not acting at all.'

It was an overwhelming experience for Sue and the atmosphere on set was relaxed and fun. But then, all too soon, filming was finished and all Sue could do was wait for spring 2013 when it would finally air.

She kept herself busy with various smaller projects but all she could really think about was *Heading Out* and how it would be received. The story revolved around Sara (played by Sue) a

40-year-old lesbian vet with a pathological fear of coming out to her parents.

Her friends issue her an ultimatum: either she tell her parents she is gay, or they will. The next five episodes built towards the moment of truth. The comedy based itself around the awkwardness of coming out and the wide gap that can exist between parents and their gay offspring.

'Parents care deeply,' she explained to *The Daily Telegraph*. 'So kids fear they'll panic at the news and imagine a future that's all unhappiness. They withhold the information about their sexuality, which makes them seem withdrawn and sad, whereas, privately, they could be having a wonderful, same-sex relationship and be extremely happy. So there's a disconnect and a lot of misinformation flying about. I used a lot of that in *Heading Out*.'

The Sue who spoke to the media to publicise the show in early 2013 was very different to the Sue of previous years. After having come through so much, she was now peaceful, calm and much more relaxed about herself and discussing her sexuality. She was still single since splitting from Kate and was in no hurry to become attached.

'It's that confidence thing again,' she told the *Daily Telegraph* just before the first episode of *Heading Out* aired. 'I've reached a stage where I can say I'm OK on my own. And though I'm not a supermodel or anything, I've always managed to meet people and have faith that I will again. It will happen when the time is right, so there's no need to panic.'

And she was more comfortable with her appearance too, something which inexplicably she'd never been too keen on. Over the years she had consistently referred to herself as 'a bit of a speccy weirdo' or 'no supermodel', but she had now got to the point where she didn't care.

'People have tried to glam me up over the years, but it just doesn't work,' she told the *Daily Mail*. 'I can put on a £1,000 item of clothing and make it look a mess. Let's face it, I'm not a looker. I'm a scruff. But I have embraced my scruffiness. We're happy together. I make no bones about the fact that I'm over 40. I don't look great. I'm a bit ramshackle. I'm not fashionable. I'll go on panel shows looking like I've been dragged through a hedge backwards. I find having my hair and make-up done beyond annoying. Yet, I'm employed. So you can draw from that, I suppose, that although television is quite keen on fairly ornate women presenting their flagship shows, they also let women like me, of average or below looks, slip through the net.'

She had done so much more than 'slip through the net' – she was now one of the most in-demand presenters in Britain. And now that she had taken steps to overcome her fear of failure, she seemed a much more contented person in general.

'I'm still not blessed with self-confidence,' she admitted in the same interview, speaking in wider terms about her career. 'I still think, pretty much every day, that this will be the day I'm found out.'

But of course, the fact that her stock had so dramatically risen, just like the cakes on the show that made her, certainly added to her confidence – as did the fact that she had persuaded the BBC to commission her very own show.

She had also come through a great deal of personal introspection and felt a great deal more comfortable with who she was. The recent influx of high profile lesbians like Mary Portas and Clare Balding grabbing prime-time TV slots had helped too.

'I didn't set out to write something zeitgeisty,' she told *Reader's Digest*, speaking more explicitly about her sexuality than she ever had before. 'But maybe the timing was right because we're getting to that stage where, culturally, it doesn't matter whether someone is gay or not, and maybe we should have programmes that reflect that.

She continued: 'When you look at other gay dramas like, say, *Queer As Folk*, they were set in entirely gay communities. But I wanted to write something where the central character was part of society at large, and where being gay is the same as being heterosexual. We're all dealing with the same things – money problems, relationships, ageing. If you're in love and it's unrequited, that's painful. Full stop. I also wanted Sara to be the only person in the comedy who had a problem with her sexuality. Everyone else is saying, "Oh, for goodness' sake. Just get over it".

'I think the fact that I'm gay is about the 47th most interesting thing about me,' she added, 'and I'd like Sara to have the same trajectory. I didn't really intend to make a political statement with the show, but if there is one, that would be it.'

She was aware that viewers would see the show as largely autobiographical, and while she denied that it was, she did admit that she was inspired by her own experiences and strongly identified with her character.

'It's semi-autobiographical,' she told *Time Out*. 'Bits of me and bits not. I put her into more extreme situations than I'd get in myself. Life doesn't usually throw up a catechism of pun-inducing scenarios. But there's a kind of sweetness and honesty to the piece that I hope is me.'

She was very realistic about what viewers were going to think, and open about the similarities between her and Sara.

'People are going to want to know about my experience, and they're going to assume overwhelmingly that the character is me,' she told *The Daily Mail*. 'I do have a lot of sympathy for the character because I've known people who've been in her situation. But I told my parents a long time ago and they're very supportive. Ideally, we'll get to a point where a person doesn't feel they have to make a statement about their sexuality at all.'

Speaking in the very same week in which MPs voted to allow gay marriage, her message, delivered through *The Daily Mail* interview, seemed very relevant. 'I wanted to point out that, in this day and age, there are so many bigger ways of defining a human being than by which gender they go to bed with. But I didn't want to do it in a tub-thumping, preachy way. I wanted to do it with jokes because laughter, if you ask me, is always a more effective way of getting the message across.'

She was adamant that *Heading Out* was not a 'gay sitcom'. 'It's using the gay thing as a prism to talk about the fact that, however old you are, whenever you go to your parents you're still a child,' she explained to *Time Out*. 'Coming out to your parents is more about saying "I'm having sex" than anything else. Straight people don't have to do that, and it's really icky.

'It's sort of, "Er, why would I ever tell you that under normal circumstances?"' she added in the same interview. 'It's about the awkwardness of the parent-child dynamic and the fear of disappointing them, rather than the sexuality issue, which is just another thing like breathing.'

But she conceded that it wasn't the kind of thing she could have written a decade before – partly because she was too concerned about paying the mortgage back then, but also because she didn't believe that a sitcom with a gay central character would have fitted into the warm, funny and accessible TV niche she had settled into.

'I think society would have seen it as incendiary ten years ago,' she mused in the *Daily Mail*. 'But I hope attitudes have changed. I'll be disappointed if people see it as a "gay sitcom". It's just a sitcom about a character who happens to be gay.'

It was also a chance for Sue to be a little more serious than usual, and to present issues to the public that she had previously struggled to open up about.

'It's something that puts me, my life, my world, firmly in the mainstream,' she told *Time Out*. 'A lot of gay comedies and drama exist in an exclusively gay milieu and I don't recognise that. This sitcom is about how we all fuck up occasionally. Not just our sexuality. The heroes are the true friends who go, "Oh, for God's sake! It's time to sort yourself out!"'

In the end, *Heading Out* was received with mixed reviews, which was no bad thing. Sue had written, produced, starred in and even written the score for the show – and that was a phenomenal achievement in itself.

People laughed at the gags, which were well written, well timed and well performed and although she perhaps wasn't entirely convincing as a vet, Sue was very convincing as Sara. Her knowledge of animal physiology was, as she admitted, 'seriously limited'.

She was a doting owner to Pickle and Parker so she was used to 'dealing with vomit and faeces', but did she research the role enough to perform the Heimlich manoeuvre on a choking cat?

'God no!' she told the *Daily Telegraph*. 'I set the show in a vet's surgery because it's got to be somewhere, and you do get a big range of believable characters using vets – anyone can own a gerbil. But it was mooted that I do some research, and I sort of forgot about that bit. We did have a veterinary nurse in attendance when we filmed the opening scene where Sara puts a cat to sleep, though. She talked me through exactly how it's done. If I'm honest, killing a cat is quite a brave way to start a sitcom, don't you think? Although, of course, no animals were actually hurt in the making of *Heading Out*.'

Mel's turn as Ivanka, the wife of a Russian oligarch with an impotent dog, was also inspired, as Sue explained in the same interview. 'She has a pedigree borzoi that she wants to put out to stud, but it's impotent,' Sue explained. 'So she offers me a huge amount of money to somehow get it "excited".'

The show was regarded as typical Perkins humour and no one could deny it was pleasantly and harmlessly funny.

'Perkins' script is sprightly and her presence is somehow reassuring – awkward but always amiable,' wrote Toby Dantzic in the *Daily Telegraph*.

'Viewers nervous about this being a "lesbian sitcom" were probably waiting for one of them [Sara/Sue] to announce that they were gay, but nobody needed to because the writing and acting were nuanced and true,' said the *Radio Times*. 'Sara and Sue were both out of their comfort zone – and rising to the challenge.'

Scotland on Sunday's Aidan Smith mused that, '*Heading Out* has got absolutely everyone in it – comedy dependables from *The Thick Of It*, *Green Wing* and *Drop the Dead Donkey* of fond memory, plus lovely Shelley Conn out of *Mistresses* – and maybe I'll stick with it. One shouldn't be too quick to judge.'

While Robert Epstein in the *Independent on Sunday*, summarised: 'Fortunately, Sue Perkins, she of the endless witty one-liners on *The Great British Bake Off*, not only stars as Sara, but also writes, which elevates *Heading Out* to watchable status. OK, it isn't about to blow anyone's mind, but it's blessed with beautifully written, unexpected lines and Perkins' ability to be droll and vulnerable at the same time.'

It may not have been recommissioned for a second series but Sue had done what she set out to achieve and more. She had taken a risk and come out of it better off.

'It's a big gamble,' she had admitted to the *Daily Mail* days before the first episode aired. 'One comedy producer told me I was mad. I had a "safe" TV career fronting *Bake Off*. Why rock the boat? I know I could be gearing up for big disappointment. But it was something I had to do. It's the first sitcom I've written and it's the most "me" piece of work. It's also the thing I'm most proud of.'

CHAPTER 27

CONTROVERSIES AND AWARDS

*'This is the first time that we've been recognised for the
idiocy that we peddle as a double act.'*
Sue Perkins, *'Attitude Awards' acceptance speech*

'It was a cracker of a final,' said Mel in *the Daily Mail,* when filming finished on series four of *The Great British Bake Off* in spring 2013. 'There were about 200 people there, with a coconut shy, candyfloss and stalls. The weather was incredible, unlike last year when there was a bunch of sad people in cagoules.'

This year the team, who often felt the cold when filming outdoors in the British springtime, had discovered heated belts for filming during the chillier weekends, which they were overjoyed about. 'We discovered these things called hot trusses,' explained Mel. 'I was a big fan. They keep your stomach in as well, which is useful as the series goes on.'

At one point it had been so cold in the grounds of Harptree Court that Mary Berry had donned a bomber jacket for filming – a colourful floral number from Zara, which sold out in their stores as soon as the episode aired. 'The petite chef is already known as the queen of baking and now it looks like she might be becoming the queen of mature style,' declared the *Daily Mail*.

The show was now so wildly popular that it was making a 78-year-old woman a style icon – already the Queen of Bakes and Cakes, Mary was now being heralded a fashion goddess all over the country's social media. And in fact, the whole cast were fast on their way to becoming British institutions.

As *The Daily Mail* wrote: 'Judge Paul Hollywood… has become the housewife's heart-throb, the wondrous Mary Berry is a national treasure and, as for Mel and Sue, well, they're the buttercream icing holding it all together.'

The gang was also now so close that they teased each other mercilessly. 'We call her Bez or Bezzer most of the time,' Mel said of Mary in an interview with the gang in *The Observer*. 'Or Mucky Mary,' added Sue, 'or Dirty Bezzer. Bezzer pretends to be interested in what the bakers have made but the only question on her mind really is: "Is there a bit of alcohol here that I can get my hands on? A bit of rum?"'

Even Hollywood joined in the ribbing in the interview, an inevitable twinkle in his icy blue eyes. 'Oh yes! Mary loves nothing better than taking all the bakers out for a drink and playing darts with them.' Mary just looked defeatedly at the *Observer* journalist, as if she had lost control of three naughty toddlers. 'Will you please behave!' she scolded. 'Don't pay any attention to them, I've never played darts in my life!'

It was clear that the foursome had definitely got into a rhythm during the long weekends they all spent filming together. It took two 12-hour days to film one episode and 10 weeks to film a series, which means that each year the foursome had a punishing filming schedule. The whole process would have been much more difficult if relations between the four presenters were less harmonious. But, like the show itself, they were all very nice people and there was no animosity between them – no simmering tension behind the scenes. In fact, between takes, while the bakers were hard at work, Mel, Sue, Paul and Mary watched television series' box sets together to pass the time – such as *Mad Men* and *Breaking Bad*.

'Mary loves Jeremy Kyle,' Sue revealed to Jonathan Ross. 'We got her into Jeremy Kyle. And she says "Isn't this extraordinary, it's absolutely marvellous", and then after a while we'll say, "it is real", and she'll go "Is it really? Extraordinary!"'

They were like one big happy family, and how could they not be with all those sweet treats around? 'They are extremely close,' Mel told the *Daily Telegraph* about Mary and Paul. 'She's like a mother to a slightly pesky son. Paul is never wrong, it's very annoying. He is like Simon Cowell; he knows his onions.'

In the interview, she described Mary as '… an extraordinary woman, stoic, no-messing. She admitted to Sue and I – I'm sure she won't mind me saying – that she went to Pasha, one of the biggest nightclubs in Ibiza. She had a great time.'

'She's so long-suffering,' added Sue. 'We treat her so badly. You can corral Mary into saying the most appalling things. I'll talk about seeds: "Do you like sesame?" "No" "Do you like pumpkin?" "No"… and she'll eventually say, "I don't like the taste of seed in my mouth".'

Paul regularly tried out martial arts moves on Sue between takes, and sometimes just before filming segments, which often made composing herself to speak very difficult. Mel and Sue bickered and teased each other like they always had, and tried to learn how to bake better themselves.

'Sue has actually baked for me,' Paul revealed to *The Lancashire Evening Post*. 'She used that really good cookbook – er, *How to Bake by Paul Hollywood*,' he joked. 'She made lots of things while we were recording this year's *Bake Off*. She'd come out really proud – and completely covered in flour – but she's a really good baker. The most memorable thing Sue made for me was a Sally Lunn bun. She covered it in icing and the icing didn't drip. It was really good.'

Meanwhile, Mary was becoming very impressed at Mel's efforts. 'Mel does quite a lot of baking at home because she's got two little girls. She's a very keen baker,' she said. And she was also clearly grateful to have both her and Sue around. 'It really does help having Mel and Sue around the contestants because Paul and I don't get involved in any way with the bakers. We're always in another hotel and we don't sit with them at lunch. We can't hear about their families and how nice it would be if they won. We have to remain separate.'

As well as their close relationship with each other, the presenters grew to know what to expect from the show too, and especially from its contestants.

'The men often try to be a bit flash,' Mel explained to the *Radio Times*. 'In the first series, one guy made a forest floor with individual chocolate leaves, chocolate mushrooms and chocolate hanging vines. It was stunning but the cake was dry.'

Sue added in the same interview: 'They'll insist on doing their own interpretation of a lemon meringue pie – what possible interpretation can there be? – or else a "deconstructed" sponge, ie a pile of cream and a boring sponge with a puddle of jam on the side. We let them have their moment but you might spot the odd bit of eye-rolling.'

And they also knew how seriously people were now taking the subject of baking, so they were very careful about what they said on the show – Mel and Sue were particular about what they shared concerning the history of the cakes the contestants were baking, while Mary and Paul had to be absolutely sure that what they were saying about the baking techniques themselves was correct.

'Paul Hollywood and Mary Berry have to be really careful to check, double-check, triple-check that what they're saying is watertight,' said Mel in a *Radio Times* interview. 'People take it terribly seriously.

'Every week there's some kind of "gate": meringue-gate, stollen-gate, treacle-gate,' Sue revealed in the same interview. 'The biggest, most unpleasant argument I ever got involved in – and it was so vicious you might as well have been listening to a phone-in about sectarian violence in Glasgow – was on BBC Scotland. We were discussing how to make good shortbread and were besieged with calls from very angry middle-aged women. It was brutal.'

By now the show had been bought and replicated in 13 countries and had even won a second all-important Bafta award, cementing its place in the British TV schedule as yearly must-see viewing.

Little tweaks were made to the format and set as the years passed, particularly from a visual point of view, to stop it from getting too 'cosy looking'. All the 1950s-inspired paint colours, bunting and teapots blended into the background, giving a feeling of quintessential Englishness that worked perfectly.

On filming days, the contestants arrived on the 'Baker Bus', the crew's nickname for the minibus that took the 14 contestants from their B&B 16 miles away in Bristol to the *Bake Off* set in Harptree Court.

That's right, 14 bakers, not just the 12 that viewers at home eventually saw on screen: two understudies were always waiting patiently should any of the bakers have to drop out. (These two could also apply for the next season.)

It took a huge amount of skill to reach that final 12 each year. From the thousands and thousands of applications, around 100 are invited to screen-test. Out of the 100, the best 60 take part in a three-day audition and are then whittled down to the 14 finalists.

The crew had grown year-by-year, too, just like the number of applications to the show. By 2013 there were around 60 people working on the BBC2-produced programme. Producers, directors, researchers, five camera operators, six runners, a make-up artist for the presenting foursome, and perhaps most importantly, three home economists.

The crucial baking challenges were always dreamed up by Mary, Paul and food producer Tallulah Radula-Scott months in advance of each series and, on filming days, were impeccably organised.

Ingredients were stored in abundance on set, with most fresh items sourced from a local greengrocer. And one runner was always available to leave immediately for the nearest supermarket in case there was an emergency, like for example, when Sue 'accidentally' ate things.

The baking guidelines are given to each contestant at least two months before each show, so there is plenty of time for the bakers to come up with recipes and source ingredients – and most importantly, practice. Tweaks are allowed up to three days in advance of filming, but after that, their creation choices are locked in.

Each year, all of the equipment, plates and bowls are washed by hand because dishwashers are too noisy on set. In 2013 this was the job of 27-year-old local woman Hannah Alvis in the smallest of aluminium sinks. It's a heck of a lot of washing up each year.

Yet again, when it was aired at the end of the summer, *The Great British Bake Off* surpassed its own record for viewing figures. An average 8.4 million watched Frances Quinn beat psychologist Kimberly Quinn and former model Ruby Tandoh to the winner's crown, with a peak of 9.1 million tuning into the finale.

But while the show was clearly going from strength-to-strength, series four did foster a huge amount of controversy – in the form of a barrage of criticism directed at the bakers week-by-week. It mostly came from viewers on social media, but also from commentators in the press, and was totally at odds with the pleasant and gentle ethos of the show.

Chef Raymond Blanc even suggested that beautiful – and often tearful – contestant Ruby Tandoh was 'too thin to enjoy food', and the intense scrutiny was a lot for the contestants to take, especially since they were under so much pressure from competing.

Once the show was over, Ruby in particular hit back at the nastiness, mainly because a lot of it had been directed at her. She had struggled with her confidence and nerves throughout the process and often ended breaking down in front of the judges. This had spawned a never-ending stream of accusations that she was manipulating them, and that she had somehow surfed 'into the final on a tidal wave of tears'. People even criticised the producers of the show for choosing her to be on it, and said that *Bake Off* was obviously going downhill. It was all baseless nonsense of course: trolling bile that should have been ignored, but sadly wasn't.

'Despite the saccharin sweetness of *Bake Off*, an extraordinary amount of bitterness and bile has spewed forth every week from angry commentators, both on social media and in the press,' Ruby wrote in a piece for *The Guardian* that autumn.   Many took to Twitter decrying the demise of the show, voicing their hatred for certain bakers, and asserting (week after week!) that they would 'never watch it again' if X or Y got through that episode.

'So much of the criticism levelled at the bakers is gender-specific,' Ruby added in the *Guardian* interview. 'My self-doubt has been simultaneously labelled pathetic, fake, attention-seeking and manipulative.'

It was a shame that such a gentle, feel-good show had provoked such vitriol. But people took the programme very seriously. Mel and Sue always tried their best to help the more nervous bakers – they would purposefully block the cameras and swear when there were too many tears, so that the footage couldn't be used. 'They were wilfully disobedient,' revealed Ruby. 'They were really there for us.'

They were sympathetic, yes, but they were also firm, and at one point Mel even calmly told a panicking Ruby: 'Get a grip, okay? Get a ruddy grip!' But while everyone was a little shocked about the hate campaign, in reality it was a sad sign of the times and nothing to do with the show itself.

'If a show as gentle as *Bake Off* can stir up such a sludge of lazy misogyny in the murky waters of the internet, I hate to imagine the full scale of the problem,' summarised Ruby in the same *Guardian* piece. 'But it's not something I'm willing to tolerate. Sod the haters. I'm going to have my cupcake and eat it, too.'

And despite the controversy, the show was still a smash hit: in October, *The Great British Bake Off* was announced to be BBC2's most-watched programme in a decade, which was a phenomenal achievement. And it was announced that the 2014 series of the show would be aired on a different channel. *Bake Off* was moving to BBC One.

'I've championed *The Great British Bake Off* from the very start and believe the time is absolutely right to bring the show to an even broader audience on BBC One,' said BBC One Controller Charlotte Moore, in a statement on the BBC website, who had actually been key to the show's initial success.

She had been responsible for commissioning the show originally in 2009 in her previous role as Commissioning Editor of Documentaries and had supported the series throughout its time on BBC Two.

'I've watched the series grow over the last few years and earn a special place in the nation's hearts,' the statement read. 'It's inspiring and warm storytelling at its best which celebrates the huge talent of enthusiastic and passionate bakers from all over the country. It's been fantastic to watch it flourish on BBC Two and I can assure viewers I will continue to cherish it on BBC One.'

Despite the mini-storm surrounding series four of *The Great British Bake Off*, which raged on throughout the autumn of 2013, Mel and Sue were on top form as the end of the year approached.

Mel was doing more and more acting, which she loved, and that November she went back to treading the boards in a musical called *The Opinion Makers*. Written by Brian Mitchell and Joseph Nixon and set in the seventies, the songfest centred on a crumby marketing agency stumbling into the political world and thus was a far cry from *Bake Off*.

Mel played one of the agency's employees, who spend most

of their time fiddling their research data by filling in the forms themselves while boozing the day away in the pub. It was sadly a mediocre effort, in which Mel was the stand-out performer.

'Miss Giedroyc is one of the better things, but the whole affair has a pretty soggy bottom,' wrote Quentin Letts in the *Daily Mail*. 'One of the forgettable songs contains the line "how did I get involved in this?" How indeed, Mel?'

Mel wasn't bothered. She was doing exactly what she enjoyed the most and was feeling happy and stable at long last. Earlier in the year she had appeared in the acclaimed BBC mini-series *Spies of Warsaw*, and also in the Channel 4 sketch show *Anna and Katy*, and was thoroughly enjoying the new balance she had found in her working life.

Also, she was looking forward to even more new challenges in the new year, fronting a new Channel Four daytime show in 2014 called *Draw It!* Developed in conjunction with the makers of the wildly popular mobile app *Draw Something*, the show would feature teams going head-to-head in a series of drawing challenges to try and win £5,000 for charity.

'Everyone loves a bit of doodling,' said Mel in the advance publicity. 'I can't wait to doodle with the contestants and celebrities.'

Meanwhile, ever-popular Sue was constantly being invited as a guest to appear on various shows, including *QI*, appearing in her tenth episode, and *Room 101*, on which she declared her hatred of mime.

'It frightens me,' she told presenter Frank Skinner. 'Because a mime, basically, is a clown you can't hear coming. I'm not snobby about entertainment… I like all sorts of things. But it seems to me that all other art forms have something to say about love and loss and pain and guilt and the human condition, and mime says, "look there's a wall!"'

She tried to get it banished to *Room 101*, but first she had to suffer through a live mime sketch right in front of her, which was actually so good she couldn't help but laugh at it.

The year ended on a high note for both women, when they were nominated for two awards – TV Personality of the Year at the Attitude Awards, and Best Female TV Comic at the British Comedy Awards. They were in esteemed company at the British Comedy Awards, where their fellow nominees included Miranda Hart, Nina Conti and Sarah Millican. It was not only a brilliant recognition of the incredible job they were doing as the presenters of *The Great British Bake Off*, but testament to their whole career so far and their years of entertaining the British public.

Nina Conti was declared the winner at the ceremony that December, but for Mel and Sue just being nominated was a great honour and something to be extremely proud of.

Next up were the Attitude Awards, presented by Matt Lucas, which saw a wide array of celebrities walk away with awards: Daniel Radcliffe, Cher, Michael Douglas and Paul O'Grady among them.

Mel sadly couldn't make the ceremony, so Sue enjoyed the glitzy party, held at the Royal Courts of Justice, without her. When Louis Spence went on stage and began to speak about the joint winners of the TV Personality of the Year Award, it was obvious who he was going to hand the award he was clutching to.

'The award goes to two people, one gay and one straight, who over the last couple of years have risen like a firm sponge into national status,' said Spence. Both have successful careers individually but we love them most when they are together judging our suet puddings…'

Sue leapt on stage in her trademark suit to accept the award on behalf of her and Mel. The applause lasted so long that she didn't know when to speak. Instead, with cheeks flushed with excitement, she clutched the award and mumbled, 'Hello, erm... Thank you...'

Eventually, after what must have felt like a very long time, she managed to go on: 'So this is the first time in a number of years that I've been in front of a large group of people without yelling the word "Bake!" in an hysterical high-pitched voice, or making double entendres about soggy bottoms and baps and tarts.'

'I'll keep it brief,' she continued, tears beginning to form in her eyes, 'because I'm inclined to yabba. So I just want to thank a few people. This is the first thing that Mel and I have genuinely ever won and we've known each other for twenty-five years, so it means so much I can't tell you.'

Sue went on to thank a number of people, including her agent, who she joked 'gives 100% and only takes 15...' but it was for Mel that she reserved a special gratitude.

'This is for Mel, who is sort of like my platonic wife, who is sort of like my best friend who is sort of like my sister but more than that she is sort of the better part of my double helix and I love her to death.'

While Sue was heart-warmingly open and true, Mel, who appeared at the awards via a video recording, was more light-hearted: 'First of all, I do apologise for Sue,' she said, earnestly. 'Has she gone on, yeah? How long? Five minutes? Seven? Eight? Did she tell you about her extension? No, I'm really, really sorry. I've lived with it for twenty-five years, you've just got it for one evening.

'I'm so honoured and delighted to be the half-recipient of this amazing award,' she said turning serious for a moment before holding up a piece of cake. 'I hear you've had some amazing food tonight… There's a bit of a soggy bottom on this, that's all I'm going to say. Thank you so much.'

Off-stage Sue was clearly still feeling emotional. 'When I talk about Mel I get very overwhelmed,' she said in her post-win interview. 'I'm really delighted. This is the first time that we've been recognised for the idiocy that we peddle as a double act.'

CHAPTER 28

END OF AN ERA

*'I cried until my skin felt burnt and my ears grew
tired from the sound of it all...'*
Sue Perkins, letter to Pickle, Scribd.com

In early 2014, though her life was on an even keel, Sue suffered what was possibly the saddest loss of her life so far, when her beloved Pickle passed away. She was just over 11 years-old.

'Goodbye my darling Pickle – my joy, my pain,' she tweeted, alongside a photo of the beautiful beagle. 'I loved you so fiercely from the moment we met. Peace now xx.'

Pickle had been a true constant in Sue's life for over a decade. She had shared in Sue's successes and her sorrows, her most peaceful hours and her most exciting ones, and had been a faithful companion through the most overwhelming times in her life.

They had spent happy years together on Hampstead Heath, where as a puppy Pickle had chased squirrels, stolen picnics and trotted off on countless adventures through the ancient trees and blooming wild flowers.

She'd been a naughty pup, which Sue had both despaired at

and cherished. She chewed everything in sight, never came when called, rampaged through tables of food and even pooed on Sue's bed. But Sue forgave her it all because she was the love of her life.

When Pickle was no longer a pup, they had moved to Cornwall, where she had tasted the ocean air and rambled along pristine beaches for hours, before curling up with her pal Parker for naps that had lasted hours. When returned to London and Hampstead Heath, Pickle had never complained, steadfastly supporting, consoling and infuriating her devoted owner, just like she always had.

Then, cancer had begun to steal her away before Sue's very eyes, and there was nothing she could do to save her. Eventually she'd had to decide, with the support of her vet, to take Pickle's pain away and put her to sleep. It was a decision she'd taken weeks to make: weeks in which Pickle had lain on Sue's bed, wheezing gently in her sleep. But in the end Sue knew it was the last kind thing she could do for her faithful companion.

In a moving open letter to the recently departed Pickle, she wrote: 'I know you had no idea, because I had been practising for weeks how to keep it from you, and how – when that time came – I could stop my chest from bursting with the fear and the horror and unbearable, unbearable pain of it all.

'I sat there, in your kitchen (it was always your kitchen), numb, and filled in a form about what to do with your remains. I ticked boxes as you lay on the bed next door. I made a series of informed, clinical decisions on the whys and wherefores of that beautiful, familiar body that had started to so badly let you down. Then, once the formalities were over, I came in and did what I've done so many days and nights over so many months and years. I lay behind you, left arm wrapped round your battle-scarred chest and whispered in your ear. I love you.

'So that was my secret. And I kept it from you until your ribs stopped their heaving and your legs went limp and your head fell as heavy as grief itself in my arms. Then, when I knew you were no longer listening, I let it out – that raging river of loss. I cried until my skin felt burnt and my ears grew tired from the sound of it all.'

Writing the letter was a way for Sue to try and work through her utter heartbreak at the loss, but it was consequently read by thousands on the Internet and reduced them all to floods of tears too. Both moving and funny it gave a remarkable insight into Sue's life and the role that her two dogs had in it.

Sue was quick to point out that it was no eulogy she was writing: 'Quite frankly Pickle,' she wrote, 'you don't deserve one, because, as you are well aware, your behaviour from birth, right up to the bitter end, was unequivocally terrible.'

'As a pup, you crunched every CD cover in the house for fun,' she wrote, beginning a list of Pickle's bad behaviour that would strike a chord with anyone who had ever brought up a dog. 'You chewed through electrical cable and telephone wires. You ripped shoes and gobbled plastic. You dived into bins, rolled in shit and licked piss off of pavements. You ate my bedposts.

'As an adult you graduated to raiding fridges and picnics, you stole ice cream from the mouths of infants, you jumped onto Christmas tables laden with pudding and cake and blithely walked through them all, inhaling everything in your wake. You puked on everything decent I ever owned. You never came when called, never followed a path, never observed the Green Cross Code and only sat on command when you could see either a cube of cheese or chicken in my hand (organic, or free-range at a push).'

She also berated herself for not noticing that her beloved pup was ill, and vented redundant anger at Pickle herself, for not in some way telling her or crying out for help when she must have been suffering.

'You made me think you were OK,' she wrote. 'You allowed me to drop you off at our mate Scarlett's farm and leave you there for weeks while I went away working, thinking that all was well. Yet it wasn't, was it? The cancer fire was already lit, sweeping through your body, laying waste to it while my back was turned.

'I look back at photos sent to me whilst I was away from you, and I can see it now – that faint dimming of the eyes, the gentle slackening of muscle. The tiniest, tiniest changes in that cashmere fur of yours. It haunts me still. Had I been there, I would have noticed, would I not? Me, your anxious guardian and keeper of eleven-and-a-half years.'

It was when Sue came back from the work trip away that she had found the lump on Pickle's neck – the size of a lemon, wrapped around her lymph. It was the third time that Pickle had struggled with cancer, and at first, Sue had been optimistic: she took her back to the home they had shared in Cornwall, the place that they'd had the most fun times and made the best memories, and Sue willed her to live. Sue still had the idyllic farm property, despite having moved to London during the split from Kate.

'You allowed me, for a while at least, to believe that nothing was wrong,' she wrote. 'We rose at sunset, in the light of those Disney-pink skies, and walked the ancient tracks together – before you got bored and veered off, full tilt, in search of the latest scent.

'But your lies could only carry you so far before your body gave you away. I saw your chest starting to heave when you took a breath at night. Your bark became hoarse. You no longer tore around the house causing havoc. You were biddable (you were never biddable), you ate slowly (oh, don't be ridiculous).

'Yet still, the denial. Forgive me for that. After all, we'd beaten it before, you and I. Twice. Even when the vet told me your lungs were hung with cancerous cobwebs and there was nothing more to be done, I went out and started doing. I sped to the health food store and returned with tinctures and unguents and capsules. And there you were, having to eat your precious last dinners covered in the dusty yellow pall of turmeric and a slick of Omega 3s. So silly. So silly, in retrospect. I should have let you eat cake and biscuits and toast and porridge. But I thought I could save you. I really thought I could.'

Sue found it hard to believe that her boundless ball of energy could be sick: Pickle still ran, jumped and played every day. She still leapt into the car boot effortlessly after walks, despite being 80 years-old in human years. Surely she would be fine?

'I didn't ever believe that something as alive as you could ever succumb to something as ordinary as death,' she wrote. 'And then, I got it. You were doing it all for me. You were dragging yourself into the light, every morning, for me. All of it. For me. And as fierce and possessive as my love was, I couldn't let you do that any more.'

On the day Pickle died, she pottered around in a meadow for over an hour – the sun on her back, looking for all the world like she was still a carefree young dog. Sue was grateful for that, at least.

But brave Pickle had done her job and had to go: she had been there for Sue while she grappled with every major life problem she ever had, and now that her owner was happy, successful and settled, her work was done.

Now she was at peace and all that was left for Sue to do was to give thanks for the years she did have with Pickle, and the joy that the dog had brought her throughout her life…

'You were my longest relationship, although I think any decent psychologist would have deemed us irredeemably co-dependent. You were the engine of my life, the metronome of my day. You set the pulse and everything and everyone moved to it. What a skill. I woke to your gentle scratch on the door (it wasn't gentle, it was horrific and you have destroyed every door in every house we have lived in – I am just trying to make you sound nice) and the last sound at night was the sound of you crawling under your blanket and giving that big, deep, satisfied sigh.

'I have said "I love you" to many people over many years: friends, family, lovers. Some you liked, some you didn't. But my love for you was different. It filled those spaces that words can't get to.

'You were the peg on which I hung all the baggage that couldn't be named. You were the pure, innocent joy of grass and sky and wind and sun. It was a love beyond the limits of patience and sense and commensuration. It was as nonsensical as it was boundless. You alchemist. You nightmare.

'Thank you for walking alongside me during the hardest, weirdest, most extreme times of my life, and never loving me less for the poor choices I made and the ridiculous roads I took us down.

'Thank you, little Pickle. I love you.'
RIP Pickle.

CHAPTER 29

FRIENDS
FOR EVER

'We wouldn't work together if we weren't friends,
what would be the point?'
Mel Giedroyc, *The Independent*

In 2013, Mel Giedroyc and Sue Perkins celebrated 20 years of working together as a double act. They included the years they had spent working apart in this tally, because no matter what they had done on their numerous solo ventures, they have always felt, somewhere deep down, that they were one-half of the comedy whole that is 'Mel and Sue'.

'We're very compatible, and understand what upsets each other, and can compensate for it,' Sue explained to *The Independent* early on in their career. 'It's like a marriage actually, except obviously without that stuff... We have an instinctive sense of when the other is bored, or being patronised or ignored. We're very sensitive to the balance of the act, and know the sacrifices we've made – Mel having to play up to being the ditzy one, when she's actually an incredibly erudite, intelligent person. Whereas with me, I have to be harsher, more ironic and sardonic, than I normally am; I do have a genuinely optimistic and calm side. You have to play up to those characteristics, because otherwise it's bland.'

They have always known how to be the strength to the other's weakness, the light to their darkness, the perfect complement for each other: like every great double act, it is together that they have shone the brightest, together that they have grown and learnt and changed.

Both their careers have gone through extreme highs and extreme lows, but the one thing that has remained as the years have passed is their enduring friendship: it is what makes them so popular on screen as well as the thing that has helped them through all the toughest periods of their lives.

Double acts are a fascinating phenomenon and Mel and Sue were one of the first rare examples of a female duo. But it wasn't what they set out to be. 'It didn't start as a calculated move to bring two women together to fill a gap in the market,' Sue once told *The Independent*. 'Friendship is more important than work; I couldn't go on tour and not talk to someone.'

'There are different types of double act,' Mel once explained to *The Guardian*. 'The classic dumb-and-dumber, like Morecambe and Wise; the good cop/bad cop, where one's a bit spiky and the other's daft. Sue Perkins and I take what we might call the Ant and Dec approach: the double act came out of our friendship. People seem to enjoy that, but it's bad for our work ethic – we just meet up, gossip, piss about, watch TV, fall asleep, then go home.'

Throughout their 20 years together, there were numerous times where it looked like they were going to hit the big-time. But when it became clear – especially after the *RI:SE* fiasco – that times were changing, and their double act was no longer in demand, they went their separate ways.

Apart, they both struggled. Sue managed to eventually forge herself a unique path through television and made a name for herself as an intellectual comedian – almost like a female Stephen Fry.

Meanwhile, Mel embraced motherhood and shaped her career to reflect this new stage in her life, by writing books on the subject and starring in family-friendly shows and musicals.

But things weren't easy, and they missed each other terribly. Their fans always held onto the hope that they would be reunited, but they had no idea of the success their favourite comediennes would experience when they finally were.

'It can take years to be an overnight success,' noted the *Radio Times* in an article about the duo. Now, they have finally become the British household names that they always should have been – with *The Great British Bake Off* they have finally got the recognition that they both craved and deserved. And maybe it was their difficult time apart that partly led to their current success.

'The cliché about double acts is that they are like marriages without the sex,' commented Bruce Dessau, comedy critic at the *Evening Standard*, on his blog 'Beyond the Joke'. 'If that's the case, maybe the most successful ones are the ones where they partners are allowed to play away. David Baddiel has even played away to the extent of having two different double act partners, Rob Newman and Frank Skinner, separately though, otherwise that would be some kind of double act bigamy. In recent years Armstrong & Miller (who split for a while and then got back together, like the Burton & Taylor of comedy duos) and Mitchell & Webb both seem happy to spread themselves around.

'The Two Ronnies did their own things, Fry and Laurie did little bits without each other. Lucas and Walliams have worked on their own projects as well as together. As with Smith and Jones, it seems that the double act that doesn't always play together still stays in our memory together.'

Throughout the time they spent working apart, Mel and Sue were inextricably linked in the public's collective consciousness – even being called by each other's name in the street sometimes.

'Even our families can't tell us apart,' Sue once joked to journalist Alan Greenhalgh in the *Sunday Mirror*.

'My nephew calls us both Melanzoo', added Mel in the same interview.

'The secret of my success is really simple – Mel Giedroyc,' Sue told *The Independent* 14 years ago. 'We have a tragically happy arrangement, like a marriage except that we've never rowed.'

So what's the secret to their enduring friendship?

Sue describes it as sibling-like, and, echoing Bruce Dessau, like a relationship without any sex. 'What I most like about her [Mel] is also what drives me to distraction: her unquenchable friendliness,' she has told *The Independent*. 'She has the capacity at 4am to be utterly lovely. I try, but have a wave of woollies and tiredness. I will always look bad next to Mel. She's a very kind and generous person.'

Mel is equally in awe of Sue, saying in the same interview that 'she is the most unfailingly kind person. She's like Don Corleone with her friends, which I must say can at times be trying: she will always get the truth out of you, you can't hide anything. She's incredibly loyal to her mates.'

It's this love for each other – and for food – that will keep them in the nation's hearts for years to come. And during those years, Sue wants to write more and also to help youngsters navigate the stormy waters of working in the media – through a production company she set up in December 2011 with her agent, Debi Allen, called Square Peg TV.

'I'm not really interested in the business or the money,' she told *Time Out* in 2013. 'I'm really interested in creating things... I'd like to pay people to do internships and to learn a skill. To sit with the sound crew or do the lights for a few days. I'd love to do that, I suppose, in the absence of children of my own. I'd like to have loads of cocky, foul-mouthed teenagers putting me in my place while I pay them.'

Mel also hopes to write more, as well as continue to work on *The Great British Bake Off* with Sue for as long as possible. She also hopes to take on more acting roles.

But most importantly they both want to continue to strike the fine balance they've now so successfully cultivated between their solo work and their double act together.

'We'll be in touch in 50 years' time,' Mel said in 1999 to *The Independent*, just after *Late Lunch* had finished. 'I like to see us as washed-up old hams in a home for the terminally ham, talking about the old days. I'll probably have an orange wig, and Sue will be pushing me around in a bath chair. I can't imagine life without her, we'll always be mates.'

Here's to that.